IMAGES
of America

LIGHTHOUSES
AND LIFE SAVING
ALONG THE MASSACHUSETTS COAST

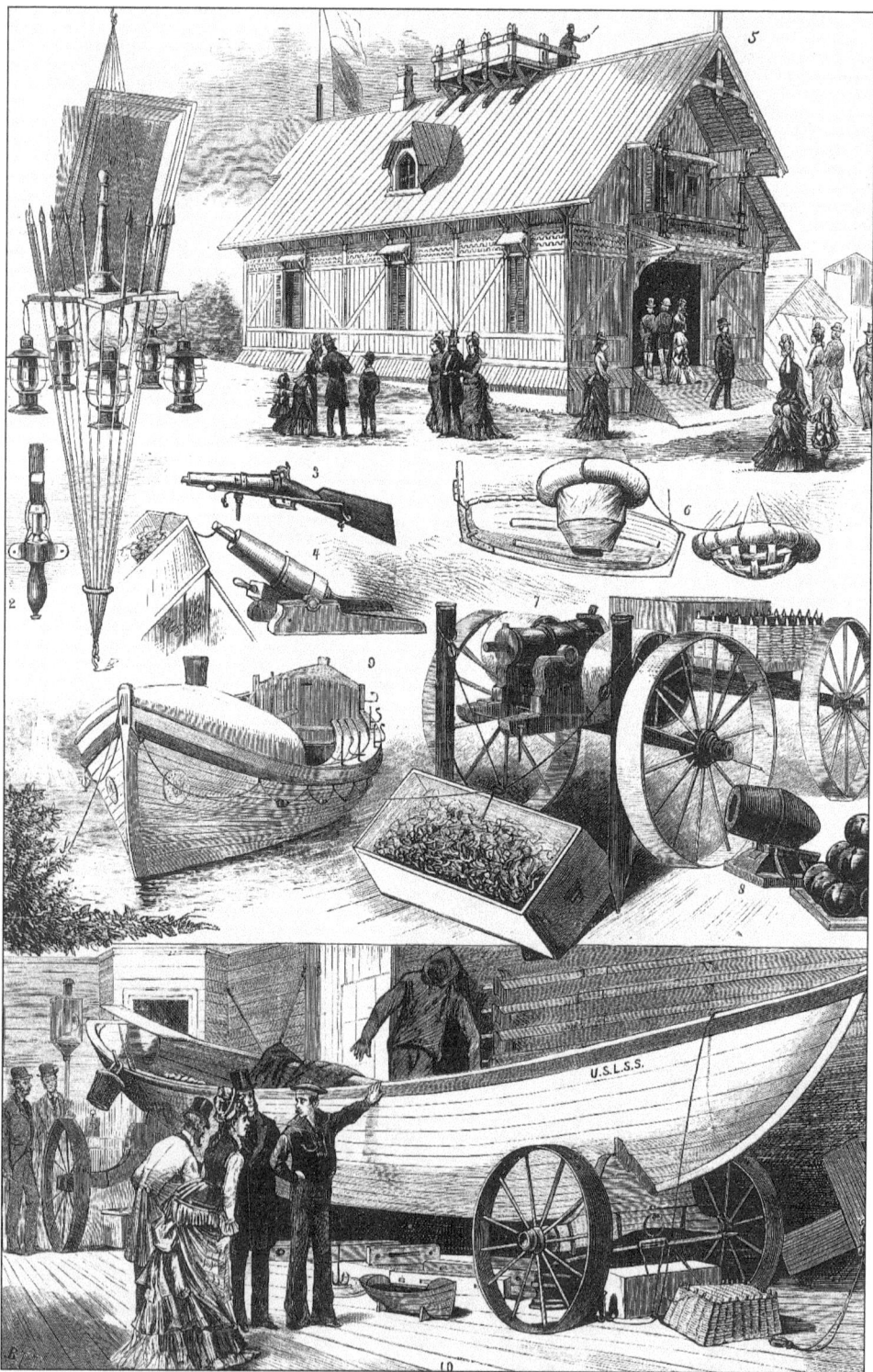

From Frank Leslie's Historical Register of the Centennial Exposition 1876, Part VII, author's collection.

IMAGES
of America

LIGHTHOUSES
AND LIFE SAVING
ALONG THE MASSACHUSETTS COAST

James Claflin

ARCADIA
PUBLISHING

Published by Arcadia Publishing
Charleston, South Carolina

Library of Congress Catalog Card Number: 98088060

For all general information contact Arcadia Publishing at:
Telephone 843-853-2070
Fax 843-853-0044
E-mail sales@arcadiapublishing.com
For customer service and orders:
Toll-Free 1-888-313-2665

Visit us on the Internet at www.arcadiapublishing.com

*This book is dedicated to all those heroes who stood their watch,
risked their lives, and sometimes paid the ultimate price,
so that others might survive.*

This is the United States Lighthouse Establishment property identification label. (Author's collection.)

Cover Image: Boston Narrows or "Bug" Lighthouse, near Great Brewster Island *c.* 1880. (Author's collection.)

CONTENTS

ACKNOWLEDGMENTS

Although the majority of the photographs and images used in this volume are from the author's collection, I could not have put this volume together without the kind and able assistance of a number of other individuals and institutions. First, thanks should go to Kenrick A. Claflin, who began the tradition. To Jamie, Joshua, and Margie, who make it all worthwhile, and Margie, too, for cheerfully working around my schedule so well. Thanks also to Ralph and Lisa Shanks, for their continued encouragement and support, for camera instruction, and for the loan of their fine photographs. Thanks to Glenda Bourque for her encouragement, her many suggestions, and her patience, and to photographer and author William P. Quinn for his kindness and loan of photographs from his wonderful Cape Cod collection. Also, thanks to Andy and Anita Price, maritime antiques dealers, for their encouragement and photographic assistance, and especially to Mr. Ken Black of the Shore Village Lighthouse Museum, a true gentleman. In addition, thanks should go to the following individuals for the loan of additional photographs used in this book: Mr. Colin MacKenzie of the Nautical Research Center in Petaluma, CA.; Vincent L. Wood, for the wonderful images from his recent book *Plum Island Recollections*; Frederic L. Thompson, author of *The Lightships of Cape Cod*; a special thanks to Maurice Gibbs of the Nantucket Life-Saving Museum; Mr. John Hutchinson; Ms. Lucinda Herrick, U.S. Coast Guard Academy Museum; and to Ms. Lorna Condon of the Society for the Preservation of New England Antiquities.

My sincere thanks to all. You were most kind and generous, and you took the time when I asked. And finally, I would like to express my sincere gratitude to all of the lighthouse keepers, life-savers, and Coast Guard personnel and their families, both living and past, for you all have set the standards.

INTRODUCTION

For more than two centuries, they have withstood the elements in their isolated locations along the coasts. Their image has become synonymous with security and integrity, and just as Americans have always held a fascination for the sea, so too have they admired the keepers of these silent sentinels along the shore—the lighthouses and life-saving stations. Today, we long to remember the ways of the men and women who tend the lighthouses, lightships, and buoys and patrolled the beaches. These men and women were devoted to duty, were heroes to many as they kept their long vigils, and gained a fine reputation for their heroism and steadfastness.

Massachusetts has always derived much of its goods and income from its extensive coastal commerce. From Cape Ann to New Bedford, residents have always been heavily dependent on the sea for their employment, trade goods, and for their nourishment. With thousands of vessels plying the dangerous waters of Massachusetts Bay and Nantucket Sound, the chance of a shipping disaster was always great. Hundreds of shipwrecks did indeed occur off the coasts of Massachusetts with startling losses.

During the colonial years, each of the 13 colonies established lighthouses and other navigational aids according to their needs. The first lighthouse in the colonies was first lit in Boston Harbor on Little Brewster Island, in 1716. As time went on, the need for more beacons was realized, and additional lights were established at Brant Point on Nantucket in 1746, in Plymouth on the Gurnet Point in 1769, and on Thatchers Island off Cape Ann in 1771.

Soon, as commerce increased and shipwrecks became more numerous with attendant loss of life, the newly formed federal government realized that a more coordinated system of lighthouses, lightships, and navigational aids was needed. Thus, in 1789 Congress acted to place the responsibility for all navigational aids under the federal government. Unfortunately, during this period, economy of operation ruled over efficiency causing the lighthouses of the United Stated to become some of the poorest quality in the world. Many concerns were voiced until in the 1850s the new Light-House Establishment was formed under an administrative board. Thus began a new era of high quality and efficiency that continued into the 1930s when the Coast Guard assumed responsibility.

At about the same time the colonies were realizing a need for navigational aids, the citizens of Massachusetts were becoming more concerned about the incidents of shipwreck and loss of life along the coast. Although a coordinated system of lighthouses and lightships helped many a mariner find his way clear of treacherous shoals and sand bars, the inevitable shipwreck did occur as the fog and New England weather forced ships ashore with repeated loss of life. Sometimes, shipwrecked sailors were able to make their way ashore, only to perish from lack of shelter on the desolate beaches.

Prominent citizens of the day were beginning to appreciate the need for a system of shelter and rescue for mariners driven ashore, and in 1785 an organization to be called the "Massachusetts Humane Society" was founded. Many notables of the time including Paul Revere and John Hancock were listed on the rolls of the Society, and there soon began what would become the foundation of the American system of rescue from shipwreck. Based on the British model, the Humane Society began to establish huts along the shore to provide shelter to those in need. On Lovell's Island in Boston, the first "House of Refuge" was established, with many more to follow. By 1807, the first lifeboat station would be established by the Society and was provided with a first-class, 30-foot whaleboat to be manned by ten volunteers. Many rescues were performed using this boat and the die was cast. By the 1870s, the Massachusetts system had grown to over 70 stations, but just as with the lighthouses, a more efficient and coordinated system was needed as our maritime trade continued to expand.

After a number of spectacular shipwrecks with attendant loss of life, Congress finally in 1871 appropriated funds to create a coordinated system of life-saving, and by the late 1870s Sumner Increase Kimball would take over as its superintendent. In a short time, Sumner Kimball would produce a model service that would last for 45 years and would boast an unprecedented record of rescues, service, and organization.

In 1915 the U.S. Life-Saving Service would be merged with the Revenue Cutter Service to continue the fine record as the United States Coast Guard.

Though many of the early lighthouses and life-saving stations no longer exist, and their crews have long since given up the oil can or Coston flare, their stories remain forever in the official records and in photographs. These remote locations were more than their job sites. They were home to the men and their families. Indeed, many of the families played vital roles in maintaining the lights and performed spectacular rescues when the keepers were caught away during storms. Through the wonderful photographs that remain today, we can get a glimpse into the everyday life of these dedicated men and women of the Government Service.

As you sit down to turn these pages, visit the Cape Ann light keeper proudly posing in his Lighthouse Service uniform, watch the Cape Cod life-savers launching their surfboat into the breakers toward a wreck, or observe the Boston keeper as he returns by skiff with his family from a brief excursion ashore. Please think too of the life that they lead, the standards of excellence and devotion to duty that they set, and enjoy the voyage.

The Lighthouse

Whether on high the air be pure, they shine
Along the yellowing sunset, and all night
Among the unnumbered stars of God they shine;
Or whether fogs arise and far and wide
The low sea-level drown—each finds a tongue
And all night long the tolling bell resounds;
So shine, so toll, till night be overpast,
Till the stars vanish, till the sun return,
And in the heaven rides the fleet secure.

—Robert Louis Stevenson

One

THE EARLY YEARS

The study of the Light-House Establishment and life-saving services in the United States presents a wealth of activities and information that draws the student through over 250 years of history. In the early years, before the American Revolution and the organization of a centralized federal government, the services provided were haphazard at best. The few lights for navigation that existed might be installed by a group of sea captains, realizing the need but having no organization charged with the responsibility. The light established by local subscription in an attic window at Bass River on Cape Cod is a good example of the temporary solutions instituted by the maritime community. As time went on, the Commonwealth of Massachusetts, when put under sufficient pressure from ship owners and merchants, began to establish some beacons in strategic locations in the 1700s. However, by the early 1800s it was becoming apparent that the "system" of lights in the country was wholly inadequate and greatly inferior to most other maritime nations. (Photo: Scituate Lighthouse from glass plate negative *c.* 1890.)

Treasury Department,
April 29, 1841.

Sir,

Your letter of the 21st inst. recommending Capt. Jn.º L. Wornster as Keeper of the Marblehead Light House, says nothing about the present Keeper's Official Conduct; and as nothing has yet been presented me to justify his removal, I will be thankful to you for information upon this point.

The only papers upon file in reference to this Light House, are in favor of retaining the present Keeper, Mr. Darling, and amongst them a petition with 531 Signatures.

To justify removal, the incumbent must be unfit for the Office — a man of bad character or bad habits — or appointed under circumstances in themselves vicious or improper — (as for example: upon the resignation of an objectionable incumbent after the result of an election was known) or have been guilty of misconduct in Office. (Misconduct of any kind — such as interference in elections — may be satisfactorily shown by the statement of respectable men (in writing) that such general and public interference was a matter of public notoriety, or by their statement of special cause of interference. Until such evidence is forwarded to the Department, there can be no action in the case.

Very respectfully Your Ob. Serv.

T. Ewing.

Hon. F. W. Choate.

In the United States at this time, what few lighthouses that did exist were poorly constructed and little maintained. Compounding the problem was the system of political patronage prevailing at the time. By the early 1800s, the President of the United States and the Secretary of the Treasury made the appointment of lighthouse keepers based on the local recommendation of influential public officials. Following presidential elections, if the political party in the White House changed, many times so too did the Secretary of the Treasury and thus many of the light keepers. Reading the records of the early years often reveals keepers serving for a few years, only to be replaced after an election, and sometimes returning after their political party returns to office. The overall effect of these procedures was that the lighthouses were often manned by poorly trained, unskilled persons, if manned at all, and some were becoming disgruntled with the system. Occasionally, a sea captain would approach a landfall to find the light emitted from the lighthouse of very poor quality or even unlit or abandoned.

By 1840, Congress had begun to recognize the importance of an organized system of navigation to the growing maritime nation and soon began to enlist a number of engineers to study the existing system and make recommendations. In 1852, a comprehensive, 760-page report was issued with one of its primary recommendations being the appointment of an independent Light-House Board to organize and coordinate the nation's system of aids. (*Harper's Weekly*, January 15, 1876, author's collection.)

With the adoption of the Light-House Board, a system of order was finally brought to the lighthouses and navigational aids in the country. Many new lighthouses, beacons, and buoys were constructed, and maintenance was improved on existing stations. New fog signals and light vessels were added, and many new programs were instituted to study and improve the equipment in use. (*Harper's New Monthly. c.* 1860, author's collection.)

One benefit of the new Light-House Board was the improvement of the personnel administration and thus the improvement of the morale within the organization. Experience and ability now became a determining factor in keeper appointments. As the working conditions improved, so too did the keepers' lives and many would begin long careers. From this point on, "lighthouse keeper" became an important and respected position with many keepers and their families, serving up to 50 years. With these new regulations came the strict attention to detail. Rules now existed requiring keepers to be neatly and completely uniformed, and inspections were made by the District Inspector to insure that the station was in good order. However, by now the keepers were happy to be a part of the organization, and they wore their uniforms proudly and with dignity, as many early photos of the day suggest. Note the "K" on this keeper's collar indicating that he is the principal keeper rather than one of the assistant keepers. Note also the gold-plated Light-House Establishment insignia with crossed buoys on the front of his hat. (*c.* 1880 photo by M.C. McDougall, author's collection.)

By the 1870s, the Light-House Board was continuing to experiment with new methods of lighting, new lamps, and different types of oil and fuel. One of the most important advancements adopted by the new Board was an invention by Frenchman Augustin Fresnel that concentrated the lost rays of light from the oil lamps into a powerful beam. This new Fresnel lens of glass prisms would completely revolutionize the Lighthouse Establishment. (Shore Village Museum.)

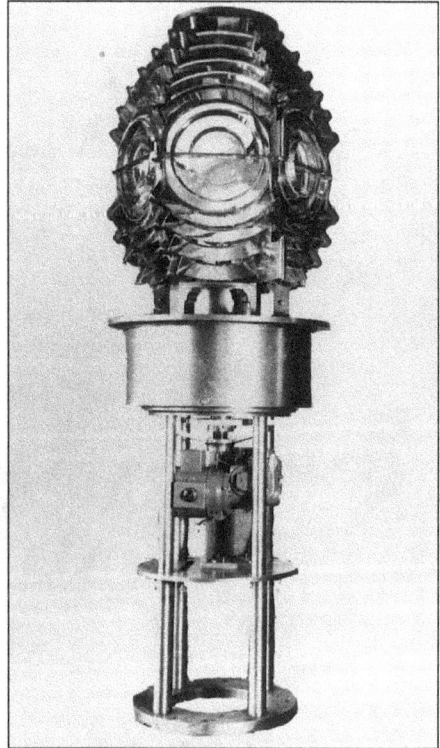

The Light-House Board organized the country into 12 Light-House Districts, each with depots to service and supply the lighthouses. Massachusetts comprised the Second District, and the depots would include Chelsea, Cohasset, Lovell's Island, Wood's Hole, and New Bedford. From these depots, lighthouse tenders would service the light stations and perform other maintenance. Shown is the lighthouse tender *Myrtle*, probably in Chelsea for repairs. Tenders were all named for flowers including the *Iris*, *Myrtle*, *Verbena*, *Cactus*, and *Holly*.

13

Much like the Light-House Establishment, the establishment of life-saving services to rescue and provide succor for shipwrecked sailors dates back over 200 years. Formed in the 1780s, the Massachusetts Humane Society first attempted to provide relief for victims of shipwreck by erecting huts for shelter along desolate sections of the coast. The first such "hut" was erected in Boston Harbor, on Lovell's Island in 1807. A short time later, the first lifeboat station would be erected at Cohasset. By the 1840s, others would be erected and fitted out with boats and other apparatus with which the volunteer crews would respond in times of disaster. Credited with being one of the oldest life-saving services in the world, the Massachusetts Humane Society had 18 stations along the Massachusetts coast by 1845, equipped with boats and mortars and additional huts of refuge. But more was still needed. (*Scientific American*, February 21, 1891.)

14

Shown are the Mass. Humane Society station captains, posing during their annual meeting in Marblehead in 1911. They are from left to right: (front row) Allen (Cuttyhunk), Vanderhoop (Gay Head, one of the only American Indians in the service), Blackman (Brant Rock), Morse (Gloucester), Gosber (Gloucester), Giles (Marblehead), Head (Horse Neck Beach), and O'Neil (Scituate); (back row) Welch (Scituate), Bloomer (Chatham), Barrus (Cape Pogue), Parsons (Rockport), Breen (Rockport), Blackman Jr. (Brant Rock), Norcross (Nantucket), Salvador (Cohasset), and Cleveland (Vineyard Haven).

SUMNER I. KIMBALL.

Unlike the Light-House Establishment, the early years of the U.S. Life-Saving Service set the tone for many years to come. Key to the success of the Life-Saving Service and its fine reputation was the appointment of Sumner Increase Kimball as its general superintendent. Under Kimball's expert management, this service would become a model of efficiency and honesty and accrue a record of rescues and lives saved second to none. (*Harper's New Monthly*, February 1882.)

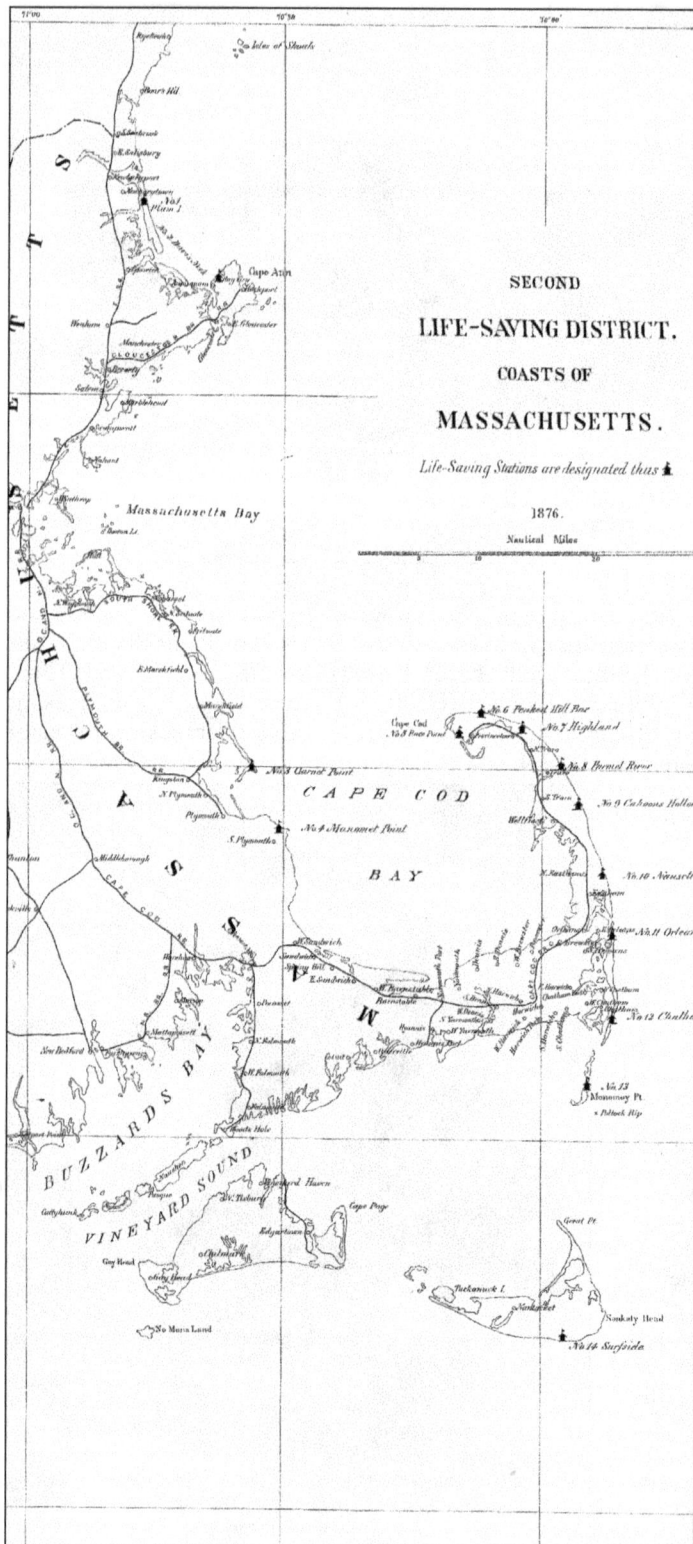

SECOND

LIFE-SAVING DISTRICT.

COASTS OF

MASSACHUSETTS.

Life-Saving Stations are designated thus

1876.

Nautical Miles

Throughout the 1870s and 1880s, the Life-Saving Service began to expand its line of stations along the coast. From an occasional house of refuge or boat station manned by dedicated volunteers, Kimball began to add new stations manned by paid, well-trained crews. These additional stations soon began to pay dividends as the tragic toll from shipwrecks soon began to stabilize, and then fall, for the first time in years. By 1914, the Second Life-Saving District, comprising the coast of Massachusetts, would boast 32 stations, each spaced approximately 4 to 6 miles from the next. (United States Life-Saving Service, GPO. 1876, author's collection.)

Life-saving stations were manned by a keeper and a crew of from five to eight surfmen. These well-trained and experienced men maintained daily watches for vessels in distress from the station's watch-tower, and by night patrolled the beaches. When a wreck was spotted on patrol, the surfman would ignite his red Coston signal flare both to alert the tower watchman and as a signal to the survivors that help was on the way.

Upon being alerted to a vessel in distress, the station keeper would decide the best way to make the needed rescue, which would usually depend on the distance of the wreck from the beach. The three methods of rescue at the keeper's disposal would usually be breeches buoy, life-car, or rescue by surfboat. Breeches buoy and life-car would be the usual choice when the vessel was within about 600 yards from the beach.

17

When the breeches buoy was chosen, the surfmen would harness themselves to the apparatus for the long pull down the beach. On the beach apparatus cart were coiled reels of shot line, heavy hawser, as well as faking boxes to keep the coiled line from tangling. To gain access to the vessel with a line, a small bronze canon or Lyle gun was used. (*Harper's Weekly*, March 27, 1886, author's collection.)

Iron projectiles were fired into the rigging of the vessel, carrying a small shot line. Surfmen were adept at judging winds and seas and were able to direct the projectile with accuracy. Sailors on the stricken vessel would use the shot line to haul aboard the larger hawser and make it fast on the ship's mast. A life-ring with attached canvas pants was then sent out, into which the sailors would be pulled to safety. (Clarence N. Trefry photo, author's collection.)

Many times, the shipwreck would be too far offshore to be reached by the Lyle gun, in which case the surfboat or lifeboat would be used. This too would be hauled on its four-wheeled carriage to a point suitable for launching. Watching for the proper time, the keeper would direct his men to push the boat into the water, climb in, and begin to "pull" toward the wreck.

When launching the surfboat, timing with the breakers was critical, and many surfboats were overturned or wrecked in the breakers. After rowing for hours, the men would finally begin to approach the wrecked vessel. The keeper would draw on his years of experience and knowledge of the sea to approach the wreck in such a way so as not to be dashed to pieces against its side, and yet, somehow still remove the sailors from the rigging.

19

Over its life-span, the Life-Saving Service built up a tremendous rescue record, though sometimes with the loss of their own men. Many books such as *Storm Fighters, Heroes of the Surf, Guardians of the Sea, Uncle Sam's Life-Savers, Rulers of the Shoals,* and others were written about these heroic life-savers as they brought back hundreds of sailors and passengers from the clutches of the sea. Without hesitation, the crews would go out through hurricanes, blizzards, and the fiercest of seas. The 1899 Regulations of the Life-Saving Service, in Article VI, Section 252, required that the men attempt the rescue and that the keeper " . . . will not desist from his efforts until by actual trial the impossibility of effecting the rescue is demonstrated." But, nowhere in the regulations does it say that the men have to come back! And some did not. (Easson photo, author's collection.)

20

Two

THE NORTH SHORE

The lighthouses of the North Shore included three in Newburyport, one on Plum Island, and two range lights within the harbor. Traveling on southward, one would have passed additional towers at Ipswich's, Annisquam Harbor, and one on Straitsmouth Island before reaching the twin towers of Thatcher's Island. Still farther southward one would pass seven more beacons before reaching Boston Bay.

The first lighthouse on Plum Island was erected in 1788. During the storm of December 22, 1839, the Brig *Pocohantas*, en route to Newburyport, missed the channel and was swept to destruction on the bar just off the lighthouse point. The gale had struck so suddenly that evening that the light keeper, who had left the tower, was unable to return due to high water, and no beam showed that night to light the harbor entrance. All aboard the *Pocohantas* that night perished.

As many gales struck the North Shore through the years, a need for a new lighthouse on Plum Island soon became apparent. In 1898, a new round tower was constructed which would light the entrance to Newburyport Harbor for many years to come. Today, the light has been lovingly restored by the local Friends group for visitors to view and enjoy.

Shown is the fourth-order Fresnel lens installed at the Plum Island Light in about 1890. Lens apparatus was classified in six orders or sizes, the first order being the largest and most powerful, and standing about 12 feet tall. Note the oil burning lamp in the lens center. Lighthouse lamps had one or more circular wicks for more efficient burning and were manufactured at the Light-House Depot on Staten Island, New York. (Courtesy Vincent L. Wood collection.)

Traveling down from the coast of New Hampshire, the first life-saving station that one would encounter would be the station at Salisbury Beach. The Salisbury life-saving crew was fortunate to have been the subject of many photographs at the turn of the century and the subject of a number of postcard series. Note that this station had two fully equipped surfboats. (From postcard by Moore & Gibson, c. 1906, author's collection.)

Newburyport boasts three beacons, two of which were in the inner harbor. The 37-foot tall, square brick outer beacon was designed to line up with the 21-foot tall inner round white beacon to mark the channel into the harbor. Both beacons or range lights can still be seen today, nicely restored near the Coast Guard station, and are well worth the trip.

Captain Thomas J. Maddock, keeper of the Life-Saving Station at the Merrimack River on Plum Island, sits in the boat room annex of the station. Note that the equipment sits at the ready with the pulling ropes in place and the cork life vests drying above. To the left are the two beach apparatus carts fitted with bronze Lyle line throwing gun, faking box to keep the shot line

from fouling, and ropes with which to attach a hawser to the foundering vessel and ferry the crew ashore. To the far left stands a rack of projectiles for use with the Lyle gun. On the front of the beach cart can be seen two hand torches and a tally board, ettered in French and English, to give direction to the stranded seamen. (Photo courtesy Vincent L. Wood collection.)

Here Keeper Maddock stands with a St. Bernard mascot on the boat-ramp of the Newburyport station. This photo was taken sometime prior to 1905, when the front porch was added. The station was constructed in 1890 and was of a design quite common along the Atlantic coast. The earlier 1874 type station with the roof lookout removed, here used as an auxiliary boat-room, can be seen to the left. (Photo courtesy Vincent L. Wood collection.)

In 1926, Captain William Wincapaw began the tradition of dropping Christmas gift packages from his plane to remote lighthouse families. Later, author and historian Edward Rowe Snow would continue the "Flying Santa" tradition, which continues to this day by local groups. One Christmas, the "Flying Santa" dropped the gifts for the keeper's family at Ipswich Light. The keeper's wife was startled when, without warning, the bundle came hurtling through the roof skylight.

Annisquam, or Wigwam Point Lighthouse, is the oldest of the four Gloucester lighthouses, having been built in 1801. The first keeper appointed to the station was George Day. In 1850, after 49 years, Keeper Day was still the keeper at this station, a most remarkable career. Note the early boathouse in this 1914 view.

Near Rockport, at Lands End, was the Straitsmouth Life-Saving Station. This station guarded the dangerous stretch of ocean between Plum Island and Gloucester Harbor. The design of this station was of the Duluth type by architect George Tolman, which was characterized by its large square lookout tower on the front. There were 28 similar stations built in the country, six of which were in Massachusetts. (1907 postcard by Metropolitan News Co., author's collection.)

The tall twin towers that mark the Cape Ann Light Station on Thatcher's Island were completed in the 1860s. Their beautiful stone masonry accents the two 124-foot towers, making this one of the most picturesque stations in the country. On February 1, 1932, after 71 years of operation, the northern light was discontinued in favor of the southern light.

In 1919, Third Assistant Keeper Maurice Babcock, who would become the keeper at Boston Light, suddenly saw the steamer carrying President Woodrow Wilson looming out of the fog toward the rocky island. Keeper Babcock maintained his post at the fog signal, keeping its horns blaring until, at the last moment, he was relieved to see the steamer change course and steer clear of the dangerous rocks.

28

Eastern Point Light is the most prominent of the four lighthouses in the Gloucester area. The Eastern Point Station was established in 1832 and soon would include its characteristic banded masonry tower, connected by a long wooden walkway to the one-story keeper's dwelling. Beside the lighthouse for years was an open wooden skeleton tower which housed the mechanism and weight for striking the large fog bell. In 1871, the Eastern Point keeper watched as the Gloucester schooner *A.E. Horton* rounded the point after she had escaped from the Canadian Government. Earlier she had been seized for fishing within their 3-mile limit but was soon recaptured by a group of gallant Gloucester fishermen who then sailed her home. (Proctor Brothers photo from author's collection, *c*. 1890.)

By 1890, the light at Eastern Point had been rebuilt to its present form. In the late 1930s, Carl Delano Hill was one of the keepers charged with maintaining both the lighthouse and fog signal and the light at the end of the breakwater, a dangerous task even in good weather. Keeper Hill would go on to raise four children at New England light stations in his more than 30-year tenure with the Lighthouse Service.

In the summer of 1817, witnesses reported that the Ten Pound Island Lighthouse in Gloucester Harbor was visited by a strange sea serpent that rose up onto the ledges. Amos Story, who would become keeper there in 1833, saw the monster and judged him to be over 50 feet in length. Mr. Story would be keeper from 1833 until the 1840s, one of a long succession of keepers here. (Postcard by Valentine & Sons, authors collection.)

The Gloucester Life-Saving Station was located on Dollivers Neck, on the west side of the harbor, and stood guard over this important harbor for many years. The tall mast at the left in this c. 1900 view was used for signal flags to communicate with passing shipping. In the later years, storm warnings for the U.S. Signal Service, later the Weather Bureau, were hoisted here. (Shown, similiar Manomet station, Hugh C. Leighton view, from authors collection.)

Hospital Point Light was built on the former site of the smallpox hospital in Beverly. The former keeper of Palmer Island Light in New Bedford, who was injured in the 1938 hurricane, returned from a leave of absence and was immediately assigned to Hospital Point to replace Keeper Dixon who had passed away. During World War II, the new keeper performed shore patrol in the area including Fort Pickering and Derby Wharf Light.

Baker Island Lights

Five miles out to sea from Salem lies Bakers Island. To alleviate the great losses to shipping in the area, twin lighthouses were established on the island in 1798. On July 16, 1879, a great storm and tornado struck Bakers Island and the Boston Bay area. On the island, the storm succeeded in demolishing the bell tower while in Boston more than 30 persons died in the sudden squall. In 1916, a new and brighter beacon was placed in the higher tower, and the smaller tower light deactivated. Legend has it too that in the War of 1812, Keeper Joseph Perkins witnessed the Frigate *Constitution* as she was being chased by British warships. Sensing that the *Constitution* would need assistance entering the harbor, Keeper Perkins rowed out to the warship and piloted her safely inside Salem Harbor, denying the British their prey.

The first Marblehead Lighthouse was built in 1833 near the old fort at Marblehead Neck. Because the initial funds appropriated by Congress were relatively small, a rather short tower was erected. This round, squat design served well until the 1870s when a number of summer cottages were erected in the area, thus blocking the light's beam to mariners. By 1880 there were all manner of cottages in the area, such that some means was needed to raise the light into view, so a 100-foot mast was erected in 1883 on which the keeper hung a portable post lantern to alert the mariners. This mast would be used until 1895, when a taller tower could be built.

In 1895 this open iron light tower at Marblehead was completed to replace the previously inadequate light. This tower consisted of eight cast iron stilts, was 84 feet high, and capped by a watch room and lantern. The lighthouse first showed a white light but was changed to red in 1933, and later to green. The site is accessible in the town park and presents a spectacular view. (1906 view by Rotograph, author's collection.)

The Nahant Life-Saving Station was of a unique design, completed in 1899. The station was located on the neck, near Nahant, on the north side of Boston Bay. Note that the watch tower rises from beside the main structure rather than from the roof as was more common. Today this building is still in use by the U.S. Coast Guard.

Edward Rowe Snow, author, lecturer, and historian, was born in Winthrop and spent most of his life studying the lighthouses, islands, and legends of the New England coast. Mr. Snow has been credited with almost 100 books and pamphlets as well as newspaper articles, lectures, and tours of the area. With his wife, Anna-Myrle, Mr. Snow made hundreds of visits to light stations throughout New England. The Snows considered the light keepers and their families to be extensions of their own family, and the feelings were mutual. Today, many consider Mr. Snow's many interesting and readable accounts of life at these stations to have been the impetus launching today's increase in lighthouse interest. Above, Mr. Snow snapped a photo in 1944 at Baker's Island Light Station, with his wife, Anna, on the far right and Keeper Stewart standing in uniform in the back row. To his left, wearing the hat, is former Keeper Payne.

The first fog signal to warn away ships was probably at Boston Light, where a cannon borrowed from nearby Fort Strong was fired in times of heavy fog. Much experimentation was performed to perfect better signals that would carry greater distances. This trumpet at Baker's Island is typical of what became the standard near the turn of the century, with various size horns to direct the sound produced by steam-powered trumpets.

Egg Rock rises from the sea south of Swampscott and northeast of Nahant, and boasted a lighthouse from 1856 until 1922. George Taylor became the first keeper at Egg Rock and lived there with his family and his enormous Newfoundland dog, Milo. Stories of Milo's rescues of children from the bay spread far and wide, and a drawing of Milo with Keeper Taylor's son Fred, entitled "Saved," became famous across America. (Rotograph view, author's collection.)

Three

BOSTON BAY

Boston Bay was once one of the most picturesque and historic areas on the seacoast and boasted countless lighthouses, islands, and forts. Over the years thousands of stories and tales about maritime life here have become the subject of countless books and articles.

One story fully founded on fact tells of the year that the harbor froze over completely. It is indeed rare for any salt water harbor to freeze, denying passage to shipping. But in 1844, the winter was unusually long and cold. By February that year the harbor had frozen over and the ice reached a thickness of over 12 inches, bringing to a halt all shipping traffic in this important port. In desperate straits, city officials put out a call all over the state for men with ice saws, and soon hundreds of men were on the harbor cutting a 60-foot-wide channel through the ice. The ice blocks were removed from the channel, and by weeks end the Cunnard Line packet *Britannia* was the first to leave the port.

The City Point Life-Saving Station was one of only two floating life-saving stations in the country. This floating station was constructed like a ship and moored in a location where a fixed station would be impractical. Rescue boats were moored in a bay at the stern, and it is thought that the City Point Station may have been the first station in the country to use gasoline powered lifeboats. The City Point Station was in service in Dorchester Bay, Boston, from 1896 until the 1950s.

Long Island Lighthouse is located in Boston Bay, south of Deer Island Lighthouse, between Spectacle and Gallops Islands. The island's position in the harbor offered it a commanding view of the channels, and since the Revolutionary War, military troops have been stationed here. By 1867 Fort Strong had been constructed at the north end below the Lighthouse. With the advent of WW I, 1,500 troops were quartered here. (1912 view by Koester, author's collection.)

Graves Ledge became the site for a new lighthouse in 1903. Built with granite cut on Cape Ann and transported by barge, the Graves has seen a number of wrecks and many rescues have been accomplished by its keepers. In 1941, the Schooner Mary E. O'Hara struck a barge while passing. One by one the terrified men fell into the sea until five of the 24 remained alive and were rescued. (1907 Rotograph view, author's collection.)

The Narrows, or "Bug" Lighthouse, was built in Boston Harbor on the end of Great Brewster Spit. This light warned of the rocks at Harding's Ledge, and when a ship captain lined this beacon up with the lighthouse on Long Island, he would be clear of the ledge and could proceed into the harbor. This lighthouse was of the screw-pile design, quite unusual for a New England lighthouse, and was completed in 1856. On June 7, 1929, Keeper Thomas Small began his daily task of burning off loose paint from the exterior wooden walls, in preparation for repainting. Keeper Small was suddenly shocked to see a blaze beginning within the wall. As Small attempted to extinguish the growing fire, it was sighted by the Quarantine Station across the bay. Fireboat No. 44 was promptly dispatched by the Boston Fire Department, but despite a rapid response, the lighthouse was all but consumed upon arrival. (B.W. Kilburn view, author's collection.)

America's first lighthouse was built on Little Brewster Island in Boston Harbor in 1716. This early sentinel would play a most important role in the growth and formation of our fledgling nation. In the early years, fire was a serious threat due to the combustible nature of the oil and the rather primitive lamps, so the greatest care was required to keep the buildings in the best of repair. Over the next 60 years, the lighthouse would experience fires and storm damage until 1776, when the lighthouse was destroyed by the British during their retreat from the city.

Today's lighthouse was constructed in 1780 on the original site. In the 1930s Keeper Ralph Norwood raised a large family at the light, including daughter Georgia. Georgia would become the principle character in the novel "Storm Child," written in 1937 by Ruth Carmen. The novel described Georgia's adventures and her life growing up at the oldest lighthouse in the United States. (W.S. Elliot view, author's collection.)

The Point Allerton Life-Saving Station is located in the town of Hull near the former Nantasket Beach resort. The station was once the home to Joshua James during his illustrious life-saving career, and today has been completely restored as a museum of life-saving history. In addition, the museum houses a wonderful collection of books and manuscripts by noted author Edward Rowe Snow. (D.J. Murphy postcard, author's collection.)

Minot's Ledge off Cohasset has for years claimed a high toll in shipping attempting to enter Boston Harbor. By 1840 the need for a lighthouse was apparent and Captain William H. Smith was enlisted to design an iron pile structure. Smith started drilling the ledge, barely 25 feet wide, in 1847. His work was destroyed many times by the sea but by 1850 the lighthouse was complete and was finally lit. (From original c. 1850 engraving, author's collection.)

The iron pile lighthouse at Minot's ledge was completed only a few months when the keepers began to complain that the structure shook violently during storms. Soon the iron braces began to crack as the sea challenged their strength. Then, as a violent storm surged up the coast in April of 1851, residents of Scituate reported seeing the tower's light, but by 1 a.m. on April 17, they heard the fog bell begin to ring violently, then it ceased. When the sun rose the next morning the lighthouse was gone, smashed into the sea with the loss of the two keepers on duty. Soon plans for more substantial replacement were drawn and work began laying the huge granite blocks in 1855. Again, work progressed very slowly as stone could only be laid during the lowest spring tides and in dead calm seas. Each stone was cut and pre-fitted in Cohasset, then disassembled and transported to the site. Finally on August 22, 1860, the world's most dangerous lighthouse was first lit and Joshua Wilder was appointed the light's first keeper. (M. Reamy photograph c. 1907, author's collection.)

Some of the finest examples of human endurance to be found anywhere were in the Life-Saving Service, and Point Allerton Station was no exception. The keeper at the Hull station was Joshua James, possibly the most decorated life-saver of all time. Captain James served first in the Humane Society, and then transferred into the Life-Saving Service at age 60, ending an unparalleled career in 1901 at 75 years of age. During the terrible hurricane of 1888, Keeper James and the entire Life-Saving Service would be tested to their limits. During the taxing two

days, no less than six wrecks occurred requiring James and his crews to perform three prolonged rescues by surfboat and three rescues used breeches buoy, with a total of 29 lives saved. For his work this day, Keeper James would receive two gold life-saving medals. (Baldwin Coolidge photograph, courtesy of the Society for the Preservation of New England Antiquities.)

In November of 1898 a storm hit the Massachusetts coast, the likes of which have rarely been seen since. The "Portland Gale" hit the Brant Rock Life-Saving Station on Green Harbor Point with such a ferocity that surfman on patrol were unable to return. Sea walls were demolished, flooding the town and washing away dunes and many homes. This c. 1920 photo shows the station after the change to the Coast Guard. (Underwood photo, author's collection.)

Surfboats used by life-savers were designed to be smaller and lighter than the lifeboats to enable the men to haul them the long distances down the rocky or sandy beaches to a wreck. The boats were manned by six surfmen on six oars and the keeper working the long steering oar at the stern. Here the North Scituate crew lands their surfboat during a drill. Note the canvas bumpers to prevent damage when alongside a wreck.

In 1811, after numerous wrecks, the lighthouse at Cedar Point in Scituate was completed. A notable story of the light emanates from the War of 1812, when Keeper Simon Bates's daughters watched the British Man-of-war *LaHogue* steer toward town. Finding a drum and fife, the girls began to play until the notes reached the British ears. Fearing American retaliation, the vessel retreated from the harbor. Shown is the Italian freighter S.S. *Etrusco* on the beach March 15, 1956.

The North Scituate Life-Saving Station was located near Minot, south of the Minot's Ledge Lighthouse. In November of 1888, during a fierce hurricane, the North Scituate life-savers and the Humane Society pulled their beach apparatus more than 9 miles across snow-covered beach to reach the wrecked schooner *H.C. Higginson*. Only five persons survived, rescued with additional help from the Point Allerton crew under Keeper Joshua James. (W.W. Davis postcard, author's collection.)

Surfmen were quite proud of their profession and their equipment. The men constantly repaired and painted where needed and were always proud to pose for the camera. Here the life-savers from the North Scituate station pose with their beach apparatus carts. Note the keeper posing near the ornately pinstriped wheels of the cart, and the beautiful brass oil lamps in the front. Only a few similar carts remain today as prized museum pieces.

Deer Island Light is an excellent example of a "sparkplug type" of lighthouse, so named for its resemblance to an automotive sparkplug. First illuminated in 1890, the lighthouse has seen a number of romantic events unfold, including Keeper Wesley Pingree and his wife, Josaphine, spending their honeymoon here in 1895. Sometime later, Assistant Keeper Frank P. Sibley would marry his sweetheart on the mainland, rowing the dory from the light to win her heart.

The Manomet Point Life-Saving Station was located on the dunes 6 miles southeast of Plymouth. The station was of a proven design similar to those on the Gurnet in Plymouth, Straitsmouth, and at Plum Island. This design served well for many years and can still be seen in select locations today.

The brown Duxbury Pier Lighthouse, locally known as "Bug Light," was located on the north side of the main channel that leads into Duxbury. The light's most notable keeper was Fred Bohm. Keeper Bohm accumulated an outstanding record of rescues including 90 persons reportedly rescued in one year. If you look closely, you can see the light keeper leaning against the railing above the dory.

The lighthouses on the Gurnet in Plymouth were one of the few sets of twin lighthouses in Massachusetts. Many terrible wrecks have occurred here, and it was reported that during the Revolution, the lighthouse itself was struck by a cannon ball. The Plymouth lights were the first set of double lights, constructed as an experiment to aid mariners in distinguishing between different lighthouses in an age before flashing mechanisms. In 1801, the lights here were destroyed by fire and rebuilt two times before the two towers that are seen above were completed in 1843. By the turn of the century, flashing apparatus had become available, and along with the reduction in commerce, combined to reduce the need for two beacons on the Gurnet. The northeast tower was subsequently discontinued in 1924. As many keepers of the time found it necessary to rescue persons in distress, Keeper Davis, on duty in the 1920s, was no exception. In 1929 Keeper Davis rescued two men clinging to an overturned sailboat and the next month rescued several more.

Four

CAPE COD

Cape Cod has been known the world over for its fine, sandy beaches and beautiful, starlit skies, and for the schools of fish swimming the outer reaches and flocks of nesting shorebirds, seals, and numerous other wildlife. People from all over the world travel to the Cape to enjoy its quiet solitude and beauty. However, only the sailor knows of the deep darkness and driving gales, with mounds of drifting snow and hail and the perils imposed by the shifting outer bars.

By the 1850s a thriving village had been erected on the sandy shoal protecting Provincetown Harbor, known as Long Point. Included in the over 200 inhabitants of this growing village were fishermen and the other necessary trades including salt works and the attendant windmills. It was here in 1822 that the first lighthouse on Long Point was constructed. The second lighthouse was constructed in 1873–74 to replace the aging structures and included a new dwelling with clipped gable roof and a fog bell tower. It was also here that in fear of blockade runners during the Civil War, authorities constructed earthworks fortified with cannons. These forts were soon labeled "Fort Useless" and "Fort Harmless" by the citizens, as they would never fire a shot in anger.

The Life-Saving Service Regulations were quite detailed, requiring that the men always be proficient at their tasks and be able to fill any position. Each day's activities were specifically laid out in the rules: Monday, station cleaning and maintenance; Tuesday, drill in launching and landing the surfboat; Wednesday, signal flag communications; Thursday, drill with beach apparatus and breeches buoy; and so on. Saturday was for wash and Sunday for religious pursuits. (Davis Bros. photo, author's collection.)

The winter of 1875 on Cape Cod was unusually cold, with terrible ice trapping many vessels. Many stranded sailors were brought into the light keeper's dwellings until the ships could be freed. Ice lasted from January until March and was all but impassable. As the waves pounded the shore, huge mounds built up blocking the beacons. Above, a gentleman climbs the ice at Long Point. Note that the old tower still remains. (Nickerson photo, author's collection.)

The Wood End Life-Saving Station was built in the 1896 style and was manned with a keeper and six surfmen. This remote station lay on the hook of the cape across from Wood End Light. When not cleaning or at drills, the surfmen often spoke with visitors, posing for their cameras, or cared for their pets. Many stations had a dog or cats for company during the long watches. The station cat here was named Tom, and he often accompanied the men while on patrol. Tom knew every foot of the beach and often led the way. Horses too were found at stations to aid in pulling the heavy apparatus through the soft sand. However, the government, in their frugality, rarely provided horses, so personal mounts would often be used. At Wood End, the horse "Jim" was owned by Keeper Bickers and often aided the crew.

Wood End Light is a white pyramidal tower on the extreme southern point between Race Point and Long Point Lights. The light's 11,000 candlepower red beacon illuminates the sea for 12 miles around. The light tower was built in 1873 and is identical to that at Long Point, making identification difficult at times. More than 50 shipping disasters occurred at Wood End between the time of the light's construction and the 1840s, making it a most significant beacon. In Henry David Thoreau's Book *Cape Cod*, he describes a shipwreck at Wood End during a mist, when after striking the bar, the sea washed over the rigging nearly drowning the passengers. As Thoreau passed through Wood End on his walk, he noticed a pile of lumber washed ashore which had been the vessel's deck cargo. (C.H. Nickerson photo, author's collection.)

Race Point Lighthouse rises from the outer reaches where the beach winds around the wrist of the Cape's sandy arm. Along the ocean side lie great stretches of treacherous sandbars covered by the incoming tides and a dread to all mariners. After hundreds of shipwrecks, the federal government built a lighthouse at Race Point in 1816, which lasted until 1876 when a replacement was constructed. (G.H. Nickerson photo c. 1875, author's collection.)

In 1876 the rubble-stone tower and dwelling at Race Point were in need of replacement, and a new brick-lined, cast iron tower and dwelling were erected. The old reflector oil lamps and green glass magnifiers were replaced with a new Fresnel lens of the latest design. During these early days the keeper's trek to Provincetown by horse for supplies took up to two hours each way. (G.H. Nickerson photo c. 1880, author's collection.)

The Life-Saving Station at Race Point was one of the original nine erected on the outer Cape in 1872. Captain Samuel Fisher, the keeper here in the 1890s, once served as a surfman at Peaked Hill Bars years earlier when the schooner C.M. *Trumbull* stranded there. As the crew was about to rescue the sailors, their surfboat was uprighted, throwing the men into the sea with the loss of Captain Atkins and two men.

F.F. Haskell, keeper of the Race Point Light, poses in 1944 on the tower stairway leading up to the lantern. Haskell's predecessor, Keeper James Hinckley, solved the problem of long trips into town for groceries when in 1935, he specially modified their car with balloon tires to make the trek in half the time. Keeper Hinckley retired in 1937 on his 70th birthday. (Photo by Edward R. Snow, author's collection.)

The harbor at Barnstable, behind the barrier dunes, once boasted a bustling trade with Boston and soon required a lighthouse. After the wreck of the *Almira* in 1827, a lighthouse was established at Beach Point on Sandy Neck. The first lantern was on the roof of the keeper's dwelling, but in 1857 a new brick tower was erected. Today the tower remains in private hands but can be viewed by boat. (E.S. Phinney view, author's collection.)

High Head Life-Saving Station was located about 3 miles north of Cape Cod Lighthouse in North Truro. The design was an interesting 1882 type of which only two others were constructed in Massachusetts. Keeper Charles P. Kelly, shown standing in the doorway, served an illustrious career in the Life-Saving Service of over 20 years as keeper at the High Head Station and was credited with rescuing over 40 persons. (Postcard Provincetown Advocate *c.* 1910, author's collection.)

The Peaked Hill Bars Life-Saving Station guarded the coastline where two sinister offshore bars wait to tear the bottom from unsuspecting vessels as they pass. Many ships have navigated the treacherous Race Point, only to wreck upon the shifting Peaked Hill bars. Because of the numerous wrecks here, the government erected a station here in 1872 and manned it with a keeper and seven surfmen. (Courtesy William Quinn collection.)

Many persons were taken ashore by surfboat by Captain Cook and his crew here at the Peaked Hill station, including eight from the schooner *Willie H. Higgins* during the March 1898 blizzard. With time, though, the sight of the ocean from the station began to be blocked by the shifting dunes so that a watch shack was constructed on a high bluff. Soon the dunes had built up to the point that the crews could not access the beach, so by 1910 a new station was constructed

The 1910 station constructed at the Peaked Hill Bars saw many rescues as well. But by now the advances in motor propulsion, navigation, and weather forecasting, and the new invention of radio, were all making the sea lanes safer. Over time the incidents of shipwrecks would drop, and soon these stations would no longer be required. (Courtesy William Quinn collection.)

to the south. The existing building was sold to playwright Eugene O'Neill, who spent many years writing in the quiet solitude of the outer beach. In March of 1931 a strong storm raced up the coast washing out hundreds of yards of beach and destroying the foundations under the old station. Soon, as residents watched, the building was washed into the sea.

The Highland Life-Saving Station was typical of the nine stations erected on the outer Cape in 1872. Stations were somewhat sparse, usually divided into five rooms: an eating and sitting room, a kitchen, the keeper's room, boat and apparatus room, and the second floor sleeping quarters. On every station there was a watch tower manned by day during good weather. At night, the beaches were patrolled by two men walking in opposite directions from the station, in four shifts. The stations were typically painted dark red so that they would be recognizable from the sea, much as today's Coast Guard stations maintain their white-with-red-roof color scheme. Most stations were fully manned from about August until the following June, the busiest months, with the keeper staying the full year.

A group of life-savers from the Highland Station pose in 1911 with a double hitch of horses, ready to respond to a wreck. Boats used by the Life-Saving Service were specially constructed of cedar with white oak frames, and were referred to as surfboats rather than the more common lifeboat. The boats had air chambers at each end for floatation and were fitted with cork fenders to protect during collision with a wreck. The surfboat was pulled on its carriage by the crew, usually seven men, though many stations on the Cape commandeered a horse for longer pulls through the soft sand. Note the station keeper in the white hat and dark vest. (Courtesy William Quinn collection.)

On February 7, 1922, the British freighter *Thistlemore* grounded on the Peaked Hill Bars while fighting a northeast gale. The crippled freighter had on board a crew of 44 men in want of rescue, and soon Captain Gracie of the Peaked Hill Bars Coast Guard Station was on the scene. Breeches buoy apparatus was assembled, a line fired to the vessel, and soon 25 men were removed. (Cyril Patrick collection, courtesy William Quinn.)

On April 4, 1915 the tug *Mars* was passing the Highland Coast Guard Station towing three barges when she ran into a ferocious spring storm. Unable to make headway in the gale, she was forced to release the barges to save herself. Grounded here on the beach are the barges *Coleraine*, *Tunnel Ridge*, and *Manheim*. The wheelhouse from *Coleraine* was later removed and became the Pro Shop at the nearby Highland Golf Course. (William Quinn collection.)

Pictured here are the crew of the stranded barge *Manheim* posing with the Coast Guard crew at the Highland station shortly after the stranding in April of 1915. The hulls of the *Coleraine* and *Tunnel Ridge* were damaged beyond repair from the grounding, and after their cargo was removed, the hulks were burned on the beach. The *Manheim* lay on the beach for the best part of the next year before being re-floated and salvaged. In the months preceding the wrecks on the Truro beach, the Life-Saving Service had undergone many major changes. As a natural progression, on January 28 the units of the Life-Saving Service and the Revenue Cutter (Marine) Service were combined into a new service to be called the United States Coast Guard. In 1938, the Lighthouse Service, too, would become a Coast Guard responsibility. (William Quinn collection.)

During the 1700s numerous vessels found themselves cast ashore near the clay pounds of Truro's "Highlands" on the outer reaches of Cape Cod, so by 1797 a lighthouse was constructed. In 1857, the present white rubble-stone tower was constructed to replace the crumbling original. With walls 4 feet thick at the base and a serpentine stair that winds its way up 66 feet to the watch room above, the tower remains to this day. Even in the 1850s erosion of the cliffs was a problem, as it is today. Writer Henry David Thoreau noted during his famous walks in the area that in some years whole sections of cliff had washed out. By the 1940s this important seacoast light was the most powerful in New England, with a beam of 4 million candlepower from its first order Fresnel lens. (Nickerson photo, author's collection.)

The buildings north of Cape Cod Light were once the home of the local marine observer Isaac Small, who watched passing ships from this vantage point, communicating their arrivals with marine agents in Boston. From this point too incoming ships could be signaled and U.S. Signal Service storm warnings displayed. In the 1920s, with the advent of two-way radio, a U.S. Radio Station was housed here for communicating with shipping. (E.D. West view, author's collection.)

In 1901, a new first order Fresnel lens was installed at Cape Cod Light. While work progressed, a wooden tower displaying a temporary beacon was erected. The new lens was constructed in France of highly polished glass prisms in a brass frame and measured about 12 feet high. This brilliant lens rotated on a mercury float, giving out a flash of half-a-million candlepower every five seconds. In 1932 a 1,000 watt bulb would replace the oil lamps.

Life-savers of the Pamet River Life-Saving Station pose in front of their boat room at the turn of the century. The Number One surfman on the left is Ephraim S. Dyer. At the time, surfman Dyer had 30 years of service and was thought to have enjoyed the longest career as a life-saver among all of the life-savers on Cape Cod, if not in the country. At the time of the photo surfman Dyer would have been 55 years of age, a commendable accomplishment considering the hardships and difficulties encountered in the Service. Also pictured in the photo are No. 2 surfman Joseph Atwood, No. 3 Richard Honey, No. 4 George Paine, No. 5 Isaiah Hatch, No. 7 Alonzo Nickerson, and Captain George W. Bowler, keeper of the Pamet River station.

Mayor's Beach, Light House, Wellfleet, Mass.

The first Mayo's Beach lighthouse was built in 1838 to mark Wellfleet's harbor for her bustling fishing industry. In 1880–81, a new cast iron tower and wooden keeper's dwelling was erected on the site to replace the deteriorating earlier structure. By the 1920s with navigation improved, the light was discontinued and eventually removed. Today the keeper's house and oil house remain nicely maintained and can be viewed from Mayo's beach. (Rotograph view, author's collection.)

Cahoon's Hollow Life-Saving Station was one of the 13 outer beach stations, covering the area between the Pamet River and Nauset stations. The station was constructed in 1894 after a fire destroyed the original 1872 station. This busy station was provided with three surfboats and a normal compliment of equipment. Today you can still visit this station in the form of the Beachcomber Restaurant in Wellfleet. (A.W. Rideout view, author's collection.)

The Nauset Life-Saving Station was built on the desolate stretch of beach about 2 miles from the village of North Eastham. Shortly after its construction in 1872, erosion required that the station be moved 1,000 feet to the north. The Nauset Bars have been the scene of many terrible wrecks over the years with the keeper and seven surfmen effecting over 55 rescues. (William Quinn collection.)

In 1923 the northern cast iron tower from the Chatham station was moved to Eastham to replace the one remaining wooden beacon at Nauset Beach. Placed still farther from the eroding cliffs, there it remained until 1997 when workers were again forced to moved it farther from the cliffs. The original keeper's house still remains, after having been moved to a new foundation in 1939 and again this year. The original oil house remains with the tower as well.

In the early 1800s, a means was needed to make lighthouses distinctive to mariners so that they could not be confused with other locations. Today, this is accomplished by incorporating a series of distinctive flashes, but in the early 1800s the technology was not available. The problem was solved by building multiple lighthouse towers; thus, to distinguish Nauset from Cape Cod Light (one tower) and Chatham Light (two towers), three light towers were erected here in 1837. The circular brick base from one of these original towers can still be seen occasionally as winter storms scour sand from the lower beach. In 1892 these movable wooden towers were constructed and lasted in some form until replaced by Chatham's north cast iron tower in 1923.

The Orleans life-savers pose with their horse and beach apparatus carts before a weekly drill. The breeches buoy apparatus was used to rescue sailors when their vessel was stranded sufficiently close to shore to be reached by a shot line from the life-saver's Lyle gun. Drills were held regularly in all aspects of rescue work, including flag signaling, first aid, restoration of the apparently drowned, and other requirements. The apparatus carts may be hand or horse drawn and carried all manner of equipment needed to effect a rescue using the breeches buoy or life car. Drills were held every day except Sunday, insuring that the men would be proficient under all conditions and that every man would know in detail his and other roles. (William Quinn collection.)

Surfmen from the Orleans station pose in 1906. Seated second from right is Captain James H. Charles, keeper of the station. Born in 1857, Captain Charles has served 19 years with the Life-Saving Service, 13 as keeper of the Orleans station. Note the number 6 on one surfman's arm. Surfmen were ranked according to their ability, with the most competent designated as No. 1, and so forth. (William Quinn collection.)

At the turn of the century, the life-savers at Orleans under Keeper James H. Charles rescued over 100 persons from wrecked vessels. Beach patrols from this station covered 2 miles to the north and south, exchanging brass checks with surfman from the Old Harbor station. Equipment here included three surfboats, two beach apparatus carts with Lyle guns, faking boxes, and other equipment as needed. (Courtesy of Harry Snow, William Quinn collection.)

71

Captain James Charles of the Orleans station, far right, poses with his crew in the boatroom just after the turn of the century. Shown from left to right are: Oren W. Higgins, Mathew Kingman, Nemehiah P. Hopkins, John Hopkins, Edward Kendrick, and Abbott H. Walker (Number 2 surfman, later promoted to captain). Captain Charles was born in Dennis, Massachusetts in 1857, and took naturally to the life of a sailor, as his father was a sea captain. After traveling to the West for a short time, Captain Charles returned to the Cape to join a fleet of cod fishermen as captain. A few years later he returned to Cape Cod and joined the Life-Saving Service as a surfman at the Orleans station. (William Quinn collection.)

Billingsgate Island once supported a thriving fishing community off Wellfleet in Cape Cod Bay. By 1820 commerce dictated that a lighthouse be built, and by 1822 a light tower and dwelling were completed. As time went on it was clear that the island was washing away, and by the 1890s the sea began washing through the dwelling during storms. By 1905 the inhabitants would be gone and the light closed in 1915. (Eastern Illustrating, author's collection.)

Old Stage Harbor, or Harding's Beach Lighthouse, is a relatively recent addition, constructed in 1880 on one of the foggiest spots on the east coast. The cast iron tower and dwelling were built at a cost of $9,882.74 and showed a beam from its fifth order lens until 1933 when it was replaced by a skeleton tower. Today the dwelling and tower still remain in private hands, in nicely preserved condition. (Mayflower Shop view, author's collection.)

On January 13, 1907 the steamer *Onondaga*, bound for Jacksonville, Florida, was stranded in thick fog on the beach north of the Old Harbor Life-Saving Station in Chatham. Despite the high seas, the life-savers went to her aid to rescue the stranded crew. The first shot from the life-saver's Lyle gun hit its mark on the deck, and soon the crews had the breeches buoy apparatus secured.

When the *Onondaga* grounded in Chatham, on board was a cargo of dry goods valued at over $150,000. In order to remove the vessel, the owners of the vessel hired local help to remove the cargo to wagons for the transfer by land. Some time later the vessel was re-floated and returned to service. In 1918, while headed for France, she would strike the rocks and sink off Watch Hill, Rhode Island.

The first lighthouses on the cliffs at Chatham were completed in 1808. The contractor initially intended to construct the lighthouses here of local stone. But he found when he arrived that the outer Cape is composed of sand, and there was no stone to be had. After a suggestion, the first twin lights here were constructed of wood and made movable on skids so that they could act as range lights and retreat as the shoreline changed. The lamps used in the towers were designed and installed by Winslow Lewis, who worked extensively for the Light-House Establishment. Each tower contained six lamps, each with 8-inch silver coated reflectors and green glass lenses. By 1841 the lights were discontinued as range lights as the offshore bar and channel changed much too suddenly for the lights to be of use. These new masonry lights were constructed in 1841 and lasted until 1877–81, when the new cast iron towers were placed in service. (U.S. Coast Guard Photo, National Archives.)

The lighthouse on Jamie's Bluff in Chatham was the second to be completed on Cape Cod. The twin cast iron towers and twin dwelling were constructed in 1881 to replace previous towers threatened by the sea, and this became a common design around the country. Each tower is identical—cast iron plates lined with red brick. Inside each, a circular iron stairway spirals up to enter the lantern through a hatch. The iron ball on the top of the lantern room roof was perforated to allow the heat from the lamps and the sun to escape. It also serves to hold the important lightning rod. Note too the finials atop each railing post. The Light-House Establishment took note of even the smallest items on these important structures and so each was cast in the form of the lighthouse.

The twin lighthouses first used in Chatham to distinguish them from the light at Truro's Highlands were of wood and fitted with six oil lamps with reflectors. Then, as now, encroachment by the sea was a problem, and by 1840, two new lights were needed. In 1841 new brick towers were constructed but these too fell victim to the sea. In 1879 the last remains of the brick towers, pictured above, fell into the sea. (Wentworth view, author's collection.)

By 1922 the one remaining "Three Sisters" tower at Nauset beach was in serious need of replacement. By this time rotating flashing techniques had been perfected, so that now multiple lights were no longer needed. In 1923 the north cast iron tower at Chatham was removed to Eastham to replace the weakened wooden tower there. The south tower and original 1881 dwelling remain in Chatham today as U.S. Guard Station Chatham.

The 1872 Chatham Life-Saving Station, as depicted on a piece of turn of the century commemorative china, stood guard south of the Chatham Lights. During this period, many such local scenes were produced on china pieces for sale to tourists. China pieces range from plates to cups, from vases to napkin holders, and featured scenes from all over the country. Lighthouse and Life-Saving scenes today bring a premium and are most collectible. (Author's collection.)

Monomoy is the barrier island jutting south into the shipping lanes of Nantucket Sound. In 1823, after many terrible wrecks, a wooden dwelling with light was finally constructed. In 1849 a replacement keeper's dwelling and this unusual cast iron tower were constructed. Though decommissioned in 1923, this singularly beautiful dwelling and brick red tower are nicely preserved and can be visited through the Cape Cod Museum of Natural History. (National Archives photo courtesy Shore Village Museum.)

The Life-Saving Station south of Chatham at Monomoy was erected in 1873, and there is no more dangerous section of seacoast than this small spit of sand. Eight surfmen are employed here instead of the usual seven, and in 1902 these men would prove their worth. Early on March 11, 1902, the barge *Wadena* was stranded off Monomoy during a gale, and sailors struggled to unload her cargo. On March 17 she showed a distress signal, and the Monomoy crew launched their surfboat. Aboard were Keeper Marshall Eldredge, Number One surfman Seth Ellis, and six other surfmen who pulled toward the wreck. After a long pull, the crew was able to pull alongside and with great effort in towering seas bring aboard five stricken sailors. Soon, the rescued seamen panicked in the monstrous seas and began flailing their arms and hindering the surfmen attempting to stabilize the boat. One wave after another struck, and soon she overturned, spilling the life-savers into the freezing sea. The men attempted to right their craft but the sea wouldn't permit, and one by one they fatigued and fell away. Surfman Ellis was rescued by Elmer Mayo from a nearby craft and would be the only survivor. (William Quinn collection.)

Memorial services for the seven life-savers lost off Monomoy were held at the Orleans Congregational Church and at churches throughout the Cape. Captain Mayo, "Hero of Monomoy," received coveted life-saving medals from both the Massachusetts Humane Society and the U.S. Government for his efforts in rescuing surfman Ellis. After his recovery, Ellis was made keeper at the Monomoy Station. (H.K. Cummings photo courtesy William Quinn collection.)

Captains near Bass River in East Dennis saw the need for a beacon and began to contribute 25¢ apiece for a lantern to be shown from Warren Cromwell's window on Wrinkle Point. By 1850 the government determined that a light was needed and constructed a keeper's house with the lantern protruding from the roof. Little has changed, and today the light remains as part of the Lighthouse Inn. (J. Baxter photo, author's collection.)

Bishop and Clerks Lighthouse once marked the remains of a large reef south of Hyannis Harbor. In the 1850s, Congress approved funds for a tower here, and the light was lit in 1858. The granite tower stood 59 feet above the water and boasted a distinctive wooden bell tower. In 1928 the light was deemed unnecessary and in 1952 was dynamited by the Coast Guard. (National Archives photo courtesy Shore Village Museum.)

As the population and shipping continued to grow, a better means to guide shipping into Hyannis was needed. In 1885 this wooden range light was erected on the wharf. Admont Clark, in his book *Lighthouses of Cape Cod*, notes that "When Captain John Peak was at the light he had a running battle with the railroad, because they would often leave freight cars next to the beacon, blocking it . . . " (National Archives photo courtesy Shore Village Museum.)

Surfmen patrolled the beaches at night and throughout the day during storms. At the limit of a surfman's patrol area there was erected a hut or halfway house. These huts were fitted with a stove and supplies, and here a surfman could rest a bit and warm up before returning. This extremely rare photograph shows a Cape Cod halfway house in about 1910. Note the phone wires connecting it with the station. (William Quinn collection.)

The South Hyannis Light was built inside the breakwater in 1849 to guide shipping into Hyannis Harbor. The tower was a masonry one, fitted with three lamps and reflectors. In 1850 a Cape Cod-style dwelling was constructed, connected by a short walkway. As was common, the keepers were changed as often as the presidents, and this station saw eight keepers before being decommissioned in 1929. (c. 1855 National Archives photo courtesy Shore Village Museum.)

In 1856 the tower at South Hyannis Light was updated and in the 1880s fitted with a new Fresnel lens. But by 1929 a light at this location was deemed unnecessary. The property was eventually sold at auction, and today the tower can still be seen attached to the original dwelling, though considerably larger and more modern. (1913 view by H.A. Dickerman, author's collection.)

The Point Gammon Light was one of the earlier lighthouses in this area, erected in 1816. The tower and dwelling were built of whitewashed fieldstone and by the 1850s boasted 11 lamps with 14-inch reflectors, showing a fixed white light. The light was discontinued shortly after in 1858, but the stone tower remains and can be seen today to the east when leaving the harbor. (C.W. Megathlin view, author's collection.)

83

Nobska (or Nobsque) Point Light has protected the waters bordering Falmouth and Woods Hole since 1828. The present cast iron tower was installed in 1876 and, until recent years, was painted red, as in this 1910 photo. In 1985 the last keepers left and the light automated. The station is now the residence of Coast Guard Group Commander Woods Hole. (Eastern Illustrating photo, author's collection.)

In the 1890s the second lighthouse at Wings Neck in Pocasset was constructed to aid navigation on Buzzards Bay. The stately wood pyramidal tower connects to the dwelling by a wooden passageway. In 1922 the keeper's dwelling from the discontinued light station at Mattapoisett was brought across the bay by barge. It then became the assistant keeper's house until 1946, when the property was sold.

Five

THE LIGHTSHIPS

Lightships came into use in the United States in 1819 and were used to mark offshore shoals where a lighthouse could not be constructed. From 1820 to 1983, 116 lightship stations were established, 19 being in Massachusetts waters. Lightships had a number of advantages, as they could be moored near shifting shoals where no fixed structure could be placed. And they could be moved when the shifting sands demanded, and moored in deep waters to serve as a landfall for transoceanic shipping traffic. However, being in these exposed positions placed them at high risk for collision. As one might imagine, crew conditions on these early vessels were close to uninhabitable, as budgets were low and the builders had little concern for the crews. Crews were forced to endure rolling and violent pitching and severe storms, resulting in frequent loss of anchors and moorings and damage to the vessels. Ultimately, designs would improve, but the service was not without serious losses. Lighthouse Service records contain 237 instances of lightships being blown adrift or dragged off station in severe weather or moving ice. In addition, monotony and the danger of collision were always present, and 150 collisions were logged with five light vessels lost and many more damaged.

All of our light vessels are gone from their stations now, having been replaced by silent, expressionless buoys. Less than a dozen light vessels remain today, a few preserved as museums, a testimony to the courage and perseverance of their crews. (Courtesy Nautical Research Center.)

A first class lightship with steam fog signal was exhibited in the Annual Report of the Light-House Establishment for 1874. This vessel was designed for an outside exposed location, with circular daymarks for daytime recognition. Two steam boilers were provided to power a 12-inch steam fog whistle, and a hand-operated 1,000-pound bell was provided as a backup. Illuminating apparatus consisted of two lanterns, each with eight oil lamps and reflectors.

Officers of the Pollock Rip Shoals Light Vessel No. 73 in the officers' mess in 1913 complete their paperwork. Despite the grand appearance, life on early light vessels was difficult and demanding. LV-73 served on Pollock Rip Shoals continuously for 21 years. Years later in 1944, while serving on the Vineyard station, the '73 would be lost in a hurricane with all hands. (U.S. Coast Guard Photo, National Archives, courtesy Frederick L. Thompson.)

Nantucket Light Vessel No. 66 was the first ship to use the newly invented wireless to send a distress call from sea when, in December 1905, severe leaks developed during a northeast gale. In 1901 the first experimental Marconi wireless telegraph equipment for a ship was installed, and by 1904 after successful experiments, the equipment was made permanent. LV-66 also made history when she received the first land-to-sea radio message in North America, transmitted from the Marconi Station in Wellfleet. LV No. 66 is seen here moored at the Light-House Depot in Chelsea. For illumination, LV-66 carried two clusters of four electric lens lanterns mounted in galleries at each masthead. Note the four lanterns visible at the top of each mast. In 1934, after serving a total of 38 years on five stations, LV No. 66 was removed from service and sold at auction. (Frank Claes collection, courtesy William Quinn.)

In October 1917, at the height of WW I, German U-boats roamed freely along the New England coast. Since light vessels marked well-traveled sea lanes, U-boats often laid quietly in wait there. On October 8, 1917, U-boat No. 53 arrived in sight of Nantucket Light Vessel No. 85, and one by one, ordered passing vessels to halt. Soon, four vessels were sunk, their crews rescued by the lightship crew. (Courtesy Shore Village Museum.)

The "outside" Nantucket Shoals station lies 200 miles east of New York and was the most exposed and dangerous in the country. Vessels here suffered many near misses from passing vessels. On May 15, 1934, slicing out of the fog came the 40,000-ton White Star liner *Olympic*, sister ship to the *Titanic*. This giant slammed through unsuspecting Lightship No. 117, sending her to the bottom with the loss of seven of her crewmen. (Courtesy Shore Village Museum.)

Seen here is Light Vessel No. 71 on the Nantucket Shoals station in 1906. On August 6, 1918, during the hostilities of WW I and while on station at Diamond Shoals, NC, the LV-71 reported by radio the presence of a German submarine that had just sunk a freighter. Hearing this, the German captain ordered the crew of the light vessel to abandon ship and sank LV-71 with surface gunfire. (U.S. Coast Guard photograph, courtesy Frederick Thompson.)

Pollock Rip Slue station was established in 1902 4 miles north of Pollock Rip lightship in the "Monomoy Passage." LV-73 served on this station for 21 years. In 1921, during a northeast gale, boarding seas demolished the whale boat, smashed the after skylight, broke the wheel, and washed the binnacle overboard. Despite constant hardships, the crew was credited with a number of rescues including two fishermen adrift from the fishing Rob Roy in 1923.

Nantucket Sound once boasted the largest concentration of lightships anywhere in the world. Up to five light vessels marked the Shovelful and Stonehorse shoals from the 1840s until the last one was removed in the 1960s. Even today, these shoals continue to claim ships as they constantly shift location. Stonehorse Light Vessel No. 47 is shown on station in April 1926 with Monomoy beyond. Once Monomoy Lighthouse and two Life-Saving stations guarded this important link in our sea commerce. Note the lantern house is still in service at the base of the foremast. If you look closely, you can see the spare mushroom anchor lashed to the port rail, near the bow. It may have been this arrangement that failed, causing the anchor to swing down and hole the hull which resulted in the loss of the Vineyard LV-73 during a fierce hurricane in 1944.

In *The Lightships of Cape Cod*, Frederic Thompson notes that Pollock Rip Shoals Light Vessel No. 42 "was blown off station so many times that she gained the nickname 'The Happy Wanderer.'" In 1880, a driving storm blew her off station, and she was towed back by the U.S. Revenue Steamer *Gallatin*. In spite of heavy moorings, she was again blown out to sea in 1882, 1886, and 1887. (U.S. Coast Guard photo, National Archives, courtesy Frederick Thompson.)

Cross Rip Shoals lie midway between Nantucket and Martha's Vineyard. On Christmas Day of 1866 the weather looked ominous as First Mate Charles Thomas took charge of Light Vessel No. 5. By December 26 they were engulfed by a ferocious gale, and groaning with each passing wave, both anchor chains parted on December 28. Weeks passed with no word until in February the crew was picked up far out to sea by a passing steamer. (U.S. Coast Guard photo, National Archives, courtesy Frederick Thompson.)

Cross Rip Light Vessel No. 6 served on station from 1916 until 1918. In the winter of 1918 arctic cold blasted the area for weeks, freezing huge areas of the sound and trapping four light vessels in the miles of ice. After weeks trapped in the ice, the ice broke up in the February thaw and the rather small light vessel was torn from her moorings and dragged over the reef, with the loss of all hands. (U.S. Coast Guard photo, courtesy Frederick Thompson.)

Light Vessel No. 20 replaced the ill-fated No. 6 at the Cross Rip Station in 1918, serving there for six years. However, it was soon decided that she was too small for use during New England winters at such an exposed station and was transferred in 1923. The fog bell on the bow would be rung by hand constantly by the crew whenever fog in the area warranted, sometimes for days on end. (U.S. Coast Guard photo, courtesy Frederick Thompson.)

The dangerous Handkerchief Shoals lie in Nantucket Sound midway between Monomoy Island and Nantucket's Great Point Light. To mark this dangerous area Light Vessel No. 4 was constructed in Charlestown in 1855. She was built entirely out of wood with one mast, a second being added at a later time. Many times she was struck by ice, and in the winter of 1875 she was trapped and dragged by ice across the shoal, nearly sinking. She was relieved from this station in 1916 after serving almost 70 years, a rarely matched record. (U.S. Coast Guard photo, National Archives, courtesy Frederick Thompson.)

The Hedge Fence Station was in service for 25 years, marking a dangerous sand bar in Vineyard Sound. Shown in February of 1915, LV-41 marked this shoal from 1910 until 1915 and again from 1930 until 1933. LV-41 would become the last wooden hulled light vessel in the Lighthouse Service before being sold in 1934. (U.S. Coast Guard photo, National Archives, courtesy Frederick Thompson.)

Light Vessel No. 41 served on Handkerchief Shoals from 1923 until 1930, when she was replaced by a the modern metal-hulled LV-98. The lanterns near the base of the main mast would be cleaned, the wicks trimmed, and the oil reservoirs filled. And then the lantern would be raised to the top of the mast using ropes or chain. The perforated circular object at the top of the mast is the daymark. (U.S. Coast Guard photo, National Archives, courtesy Frederick Thompson.)

Storms, the ravages of the sea, loneliness, and cold took their toll on sailors who manned these early light vessels. Life on board a New England lightship was anything but placid. While an occasional warm summer afternoon could be a relief, the unpredictable ocean and New England storms caused great hardships among the crews. Early lightships were cold, damp, and had only the sparest of comforts as most of the space was allocated to fuel and stores. More detrimental was the constant severe rolling of the vessel. Most of the early vessels heaved and tossed and it was a constant chore just to perform daily routines. Also, early vessels contained no form of propulsion in the event that the large mushroom anchor or chain parted, so many times a vessel would be driven hundreds of miles off station in a storm. Without engines, and with only a minimum of sails, crews would be forced to wait until they came ashore or were discovered by a passing vessel—some never were found and their fates will never be known. (U.S. Coast Guard photo, National Archives, courtesy Frederick Thompson.)

Succonnessett Light Vessel No. 6 stood watch over the North Channel of Nantucket Sound from 1854 until 1912. Illuminating apparatus consisted of a single lantern on the main mast with eight lamps and reflectors. On February 4, 1918, the keeper of the lighthouse at Great Point on Nantucket reported seeing LV-6 adrift in heavy ice. The tender *Azalia* and naval vessels were dispatched, but the vessel and her crew of six were never seen again. (Courtesy Nautical Research Center.)

Vineyard Sound Light Vessel marked the submerged reef off Cuttyhunk near the southern entrance to Buzzards Bay. In September 1944 a devastating hurricane moved up the coast, striking New England on September 13. When the storm subsided the next day, LV-73 had disappeared with all hands. Here the #73 is seen in 1933 while under Lighthouse Service jurisdiction, as she arrives at the Chelsea Light-House Depot. (Willard Flint collection, courtesy Shore Village Museum.)

After the loss of LV-73, LV-110 from Pollock Rip Station was transferred to the Vineyard Station. She would serve here until 1954 when the station was renamed Buzzards Bay. In 1954 during a hurricane, she too lost a crewman, washed over the side by a huge wave. Miraculously, the seaman was rescued the next day by a Coast Guard cutter patrolling in the area. (U.S. Coast Guard photograph, courtesy Shore Village Museum.)

Pictured on Handkerchief Station in Nantucket Sound, LV-98 was a steel hulled "turtle neck" type of light vessel. Frederic Thompson noted in *The Lightships of Cape Cod* that LV-98 became one of the favorite haunts for Coast Guardsmen, for on board was a cook named Gus who was reputed to serve the most delicious hot twisted rolls in the Service. In 1951 she was decommissioned after 21 years on station. (U.S. Coast Guard photo, courtesy Frederick Thompson.)

Light Vessel No. 47 marked the Pollock Rip Station from 1892 until 1923, serving later on Cross Rip and Stonehorse Shoal before being retired in 1934. In December of 1909, while on Pollock Rip Station, she was dismasted and dragged off station in a collision with the four-masted schooner *Katherine Perry*. In the collision, the light vessel's mast was broken at the base, tearing out the bulwark of the lantern house. (Tom Miles collection, courtesy Shore Village Museum.)

Hen and Chickens Light Vessel WAL-551 is shown on station in January of 1949. Five years later this station was discontinued and replaced by the new Buzzards Bay Station, located 4 miles west of Cuttyhunk Light. Vessels guarding this station were blown adrift or dragged off station four times in severe weather. (U.S. Coast Guard photo, courtesy Frederick Thompson.)

Hen and Chickens Shoal lies at the entrance to Buzzards Bay and has been marked by a light vessel since 1866. Here, LV-42, on this station from 1913 until 1932, is shown receiving supplies from the lighthouse tender moored to her stern. Note, near the base of the aft mast, the two lamps. These lamps would be hoisted to the top of the mast at dusk and lowered at daylight for cleaning or maintenance. Seen here electrified, the oil lanterns were once housed in the little shack below for cleaning during the day. The roof of the shack would open to allow the lanterns to be lowered inside. Now, no longer needed, the roof has had a small deck added. A similar lantern house can be seen at the base of the foremast. (U.S. Coast Guard photo, courtesy Frederick Thompson.)

The Nantucket Light Vessel No. 112 was given to the U.S. Government by Great Britain in 1936 in reparation for the sinking of LV-117 in 1934. She was diesel powered and equipped with the latest safety devices in case of collision. These devices included a radio beacon, diaphone fog signal, double bottom and sides, and escape hatches for the crewmen to prevent their being trapped below decks. The Nantucket station continued to be one of the most exposed and dangerous stations in the country, and vessels manning this station were blown or dragged off station 29 times, with two being sunk in collisions. LV-112 served on the Nantucket Station until 1973, when she was relieved. Today she can still be seen on exhibit in Bridgeport, Connecticut. (U.S. Coast Guard photo, courtesy Shore Village Museum.)

Pollock Rip Light Vessel No. 110 was constructed in 1923 and served only a short time when struck by a violent gale. Towering waves hammered the vessel, destroying the whaleboat and tearing equipment free. When the storm subsided, the clearing skies revealed the battered but still floating vessel seen here. When the Cape Cod Canal opened in 1914, traffic through this area began to decline until 1969 when the station was replaced by a lighted buoy. (Courtesy Shore Village Museum.)

A constant danger to light vessels was that of collision with passing ships. Since these vessels were moored to mark obstructions within well-traveled sea lanes or as "signposts" on approaches to ports, near misses and collisions were relatively common. Here the captain of LV-54 on the Boston Station inspects the damage after being rammed by the British steamer *Seven Seas Spray* on December 20, 1935. (Courtesy Shore Village Museum.)

Six

NANTUCKET AND MARTHA'S VINEYARD

Nantucket and Martha's Vineyard are located south of Cape Cod, in the center of one of the most traversed shipping routes in the world. The inviting beaches of these beautiful islands belies the fact that they are surrounded by countless treacherous shoals extending far out to sea. The area was once marked by more light vessels than any other spot along our coasts. The coasts here were protected by volunteer and government life-saving crews, but in the gales and pea soup fogs, many ships were still driven onto the shoals. Lighthouse keepers and life-savers alike teamed up to rescue sailors from the many vessels that met their fate, and countless dramatic rescues have been recorded. Many times the services drew upon the islanders for the experienced boatmen needed to navigate the small boats out into the sea and many local names appear in the service personnel records. Though many of these stations were on lonely stretches of beach, none was more stark and distant than those at Great Point on Nantucket.

The lighthouse at Great Point on Sandy Point was first erected in 1784 to protect mariners from the dangerous shoals stretching into Nantucket Sound. There was no keeper's dwelling at first, so the keepers had to make the long walk to and from the tower daily. In 1816, the lighthouse burned and was replaced in 1818 by a new rubble-stone light. Shown here in 1944, the light beamed across the sound until 1984, when a fierce storm destroyed the tower. (U.S. Coast Guard photo, author's collection.)

SURFSIDE LIFE SAVING STATION   THE   MUSKEGET LIFE SAVING STATION
COSKATA LIFE SAVING STATION   BEACH   MADDAKET LIFE SAVING STATION
PATROL

This composite view presents a nice comparison of the four life-saving stations on Nantucket. Note in the bottom right image of the Maddaket station the utility building on the right, which was moved in 1947 to the Coast Guard station at Brant Point and remains today. The Coskata station was moved to Brant Point as well, and served as a barracks there. (From J.H. Robinson, *106 Views of Nantucket*. 1911, author's collection.)

The Life-Saving Station at Coskata, near the Glades at Great Point, was the third station on the island, erected in 1883. Walter N. Chase was the keeper here when his crew would be given the ultimate test of skill and strength when on January 20, 1892, the schooner *H.P. Kirkham* was caught in a violent squall and struck the Rose and Crown Shoals, 15 miles off Great Point. (Courtesy Nantucket Life-Saving Museum.)

Captain Chase knew that they must attempt a rescue, and soon the crew headed out 15 miles toward the shoals. After six hours of rowing, the difficult task of getting the sailors aboard in heavy seas lay ahead. A line was made fast, and six times the crew maneuvered their boat closer in spite of the seas lurking to destroy them. Six times a sailor clamored into the surfboat. Finally it was time for the arduous journey back to shore. The keeper could not see land, and the seas were against him. And now ten hours had passed. Steamships dispatched to render aid had retreated in the monstrous seas. Throughout the night, Keeper Chase, with his men sick from exhaustion, maintained his vigil as Nantucket still lay 11 miles ahead. The men pulled steadily, and after 26 hours, the crew finally landed their precious cargo. One noble member never saw the medals awarded by his government, for he never recovered from his ordeal. But he would be remembered in one of the most spectacular Life-Saving Service rescues. (Photo c. 1892. Keeper Chase and his "Gold Medal Crew," courtesy Nantucket Life-Saving Museum.)

Sankaty Head Light was erected in 1849 on a cliff near Siasconset to warn mariners from the dangerous Davis South Shoals. The new Fresnel lens was installed in 1850, and for a time, the light was superior to every other American light. During the early years there was no keeper's house provided, forcing the keepers to travel some distance to tend the light. In the 1890s, Joseph Ramsen left the Life-Saving Service to become keeper and served with distinction. The lighthouse was fully electrified in 1933, and in 1950 the large first order lens was removed to the fine Whaling Museum in the town center where today it can still be viewed in operation. For many years, even into the 1950s, Sankaty Light had few modern conveniences, and it was not until 1952 after Keeper Grieder's wife, Elsie, wrote to President Truman that the station received running water.

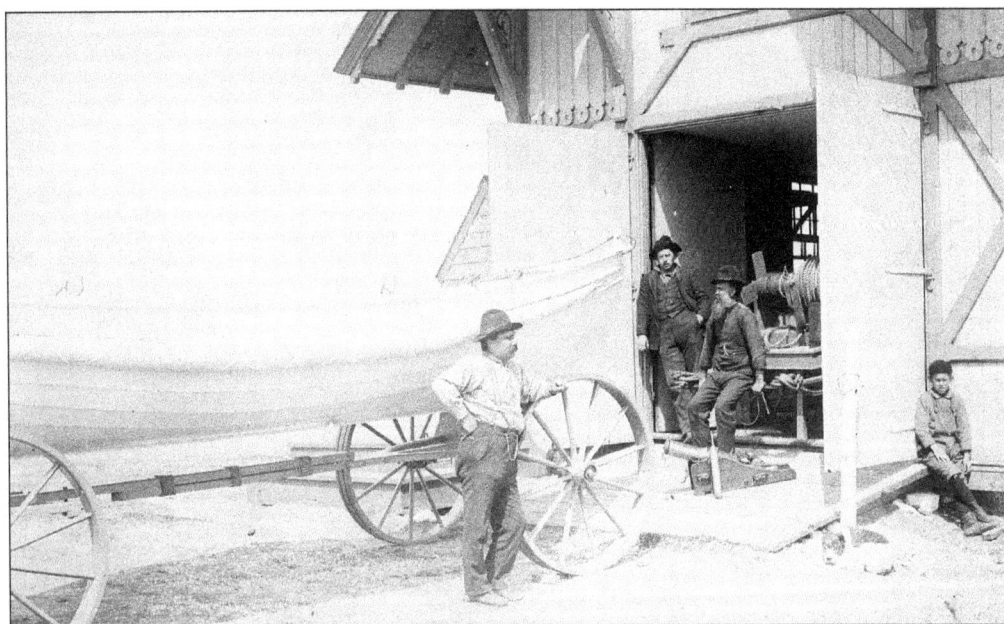

This early view, probably of the Surfside Life-Saving Station, was taken prior to 1884 when the additions on each "wing" were constructed. This early station was announced in 1873 when Captain Merriman of the U.S. Revenue Cutter Service came to the island to select the site and make arrangements. The structure was completed within 100 days at a cost of $2,500. Note the Lyle gun and projectiles. (J. Freeman photo, author's collection.)

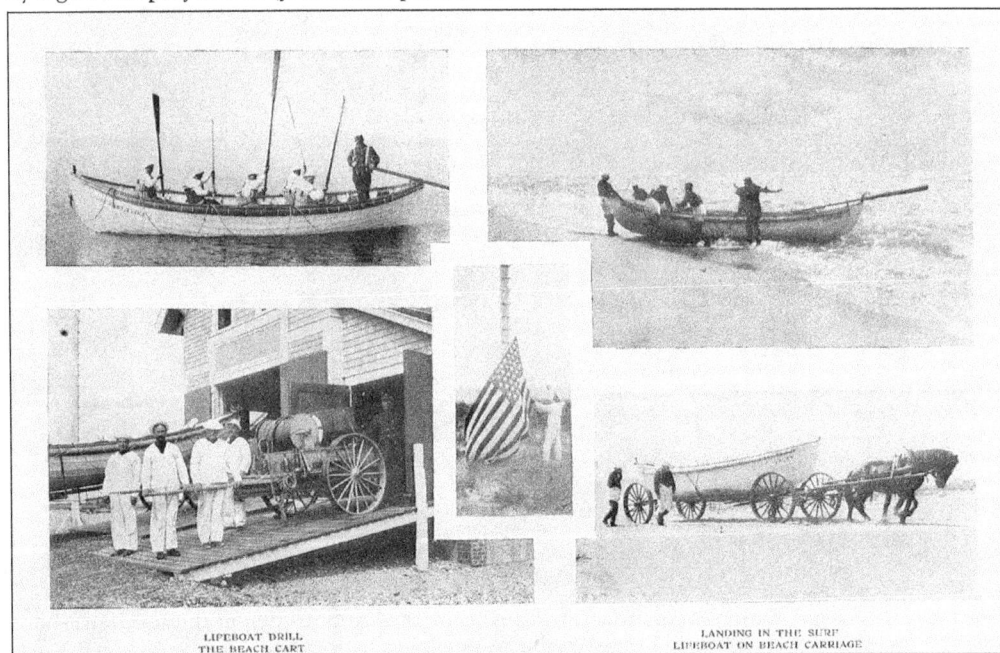

LIFEBOAT DRILL
THE BEACH CART

LANDING IN THE SURF
LIFEBOAT ON BEACH CARRIAGE

This composite shows the Coskata crew drilling with surfboat and beach apparatus in about 1900. The view is one of a series published by J.H. Robinson in 1911 in his book *106 Views of Nantucket*. Life-savers were always a wonderful subject for articles, photos, and books of the day, for they were most respected for their bravery and hard work. (Author's collection.)

107

The first Life-Saving station on Nantucket was built in 1874 at Surfside, on the southern shore near the Humane Society house. This classic station was quite detailed and a beauty to behold. Retired captain Joseph Winslow was appointed the first keeper and he immediately began training his crew. Patrols were begun, watches set, and a strict routine established. Their first rescue occurred in March of 1877 when the bark W.F. Marshall lost her way in fog and grounded

on the shoals. The life-savers were unable to launch their boat through the high surf but fired a line, reaching the vessel. Sixteen persons were rescued before the ship broke up. The station was modified in 1888 to enlarge it by adding the "wings" pictured for additional apparatus, and a new lookout was added. Today a replica serves as the Nantucket Life-Saving Museum, providing a wonderful look at early life-saving here. (Courtesy Nantucket Life-Saving Museum.)

During the early years at Surfside, the site was used extensively for evaluating new life-saving inventions. For two days in 1876 projectile firing devices were tested here, and as a result the bronze gun developed by Captain David A. Lyle would become the standard of the Life-Saving Service. The Surfside station was decommissioned in 1921, and today the beautiful structure remains preserved as a Youth Hostel. (Courtesy Nantucket Life-Saving Museum.)

In 1891 the Life-Saving Service erected their fourth station 6 miles west of Surfside at Great Neck. Later renamed Madaket (Maddequett), the station saw much activity as many ships came to grief on the shoals. Nantucket surfmen, pictured here from left to right are: Steven Hussey, Ollie Fisher, Keeper George Orpin, Nelson Ewer, George Rogers, and Maurice Gibbs. Within hours of closing in 1947, the steamer Kotar would run aground here. (Courtesy Nantucket Life-Saving Museum.)

The lighthouse erected at Brant Point in 1746 was the second lighthouse to be built in America. Since the first lantern was hoisted, a total of ten lighthouses have been built on the site. Many of these early lights were prone to fire and severe storms until 1856, when this brown brick tower and attached keeper's dwelling was constructed. (Henry S., Wyer photo, author's collection.)

By 1900, due to the constantly shifting harbor channel, the Light-House Board saw the need for an additional beacon and so erected a smaller wooden beacon showing a fixed red light. The brick tower was capped over and is still in use as the radio room at Coast Guard Station Brant Point. The light here now shines from 26 feet above high water, the lowest lighthouse in New England. (M.W. Boyer view, author's collection.)

Muskeget Island lies off the western tip of Nantucket and was the scene of many disasters to the coal fleets in the 1870s. Because of the dangers here, Muskeget Station was erected near the western tip, close to Vineyard Passage. On Christmas Eve in 1889, while the crew was on patrol during a gale, a spark from a faulty chimney ignited within the walls and the building was soon lost. (Courtesy Nantucket Life-Saving Museum.)

This 1943 photograph by author Edward Rowe Snow was taken in front of the Historical Association's Whaling Museum while he was researching some of his early maritime books. Pictured here are Mr. Snow's mother (far left) and Edouard Stackpole, author of *Life Saving—Nantucket*. The Snows were avid New England and maritime historians and made countless trips together exploring the region. (Author's collection.)

The second Life-Saving Station at Muskeget was started in 1891, but construction was slow here as the major effort was put into completing the station at Madaket. The Muskeget crew occupied a house and boathouse on Tuckernuck Island for the duration, and finally in 1895 they moved in. In 1929, the Coast Guard decommissioned the station, and soon it fell into disrepair. Time and vandalism took its toll and the building was later lost. (Courtesy Nantucket Life-Saving Museum.)

Across Vineyard Sound from Nantucket, high on the colorful cliffs of Martha's Vineyard, sits Gay Head Lighthouse. Explorer Bartholomew Gosnold first named this area in 1602, and by the 1790s trade in the area had increased to require a beacon suitable to guide the incoming ships from Boston. The first tower, probably of wood, was constructed in 1799 along with a keeper's dwelling, barn, and oil storage vault. By 1856 the now aged tower required replacement, and the new brick tower pictured above with double-sided keeper's house was provided. The tower was fitted with a new first order Fresnel lens, shipped directly from France. One of the worst disasters off Gay Head occurred on January 19, 1884, when the coastwise steamer *City of Columbus* struck the submerged Devil's Bridge Ledge while steaming south, sinking immediately. Lighthouse Keeper Horatio Pease raced to the wreck by boat and was able to save some of the passengers, but in the final toll 103 persons had been lost. (Chamberlain photo, courtesy Andrew Price collection.)

114

In 1902 the old, damp brick double keeper's dwelling at Gay Head was completely replaced with a new two-story gambrel-roofed dwelling. Today, two aerobeacons replace the old first order lens which resides at the Dukes County Historical Society. Though the dwelling has now been torn down, the famous old tower remains. (1908 view, author's collection.)

East Chop Light, Oak Bluffs, Mass.

East Chop Light is located on top of Telegraph Hill on the east side of Vineyard Haven Harbor. In 1876, the cast iron lighthouse was erected to replace a private light maintained by local merchants. For years the tower was painted a dark brown and showed a fixed red light. In recent times the structure has been changed back to its original white color scheme and now shows a green flashing light.

115

In 1828 the lighthouse in the inner harbor at Edgartown was erected. A two-story keeper's dwelling was located at the end of the breakwater and soon fitted with a fourth order lantern protruding from the roof, visible for 14 miles. After 100 years of service, the old house and lantern were finally replaced in 1941. The cast iron tower from the decommissioned Ipswich Light Station was moved by barge and erected on the site and this structure then demolished. Shown here is the nicely maintained lighthouse, probably in the early 1900s.

Cape Poque Light, Chapquidic, near Oak Bluffs, Mass.

Cape Pogue Light lies on the northeastern part of Chappaquiddick Island, near Oak Bluffs on Martha's Vineyard. The white frame wooden tower was a welcome sight when constructed in 1802 on what some call the most desolate location in the area. In 1880 the new double keeper's dwelling, shown above, was added, and in 1893 the old tower replaced by the one that stands today. (Tichnor Bros. View, author's collection.)

Protecting the west side of Vineyard Haven Harbor was the West Chop or Holmes's Hole Light. The first tower was erected in 1817, but because of poor workmanship, a new tower and dwelling would be constructed in 1846. Shown above in 1870, the tower was connected to the original stone dwelling by an enclosed walkway. In 1891, this tower was replaced with a new 45-foot, red brick tower, which stands today.

117

This official Coast Guard aerial view shows the West Chop Light Station in August of 1951. The metal garage on the top right was constructed in 1925, and for a time during WW II there was also a lookout tower from which to watch for enemy submarines. Note the 1846 fog whistle building in the lower right. Here were the steam boilers to generate sufficient steam to power the fog trumpets. The early oil house still remains in the lower left. The light tower, once red, was painted white in 1899. (Official U.S. Coast Guard photo, author's collection.)

Seven

BUZZARDS BAY

Palmer Island Lighthouse is one of the many interesting lighthouses located in Buzzards Bay, halfway between Fairhaven and New Bedford. Noted New England artist Arthur Small, who painted many New England lighthouse scenes, was also a light keeper for many years throughout New England including more than 16 years at Palmer Island Light. Keeper Small had many stories of his years in the Lighthouse Service, but unfortunately, the most tragic occurred here in 1938. As the famous 1938 Hurricane traveled up the New England coast, Palmer Island found itself directly in its track. Keeper Small was intent at keeping his fog signal blasting, as he knew that the Nantucket boat was soon scheduled to pass with its load of 200 passengers. As the mountainous waves struck the island and soon demolished their house, Keeper Small helped his wife to take refuge in the brick oil house. Keeper Small removed shelving and built a platform for his wife, Mable, to wait, and then went to resume his work on the fog signal. The keeper had no way of knowing that the Nantucket boat had already taken refuge from the storm. As wave after wave washed over the island, Keeper Small was swept into the sea. When Mable Small saw her husband in peril, she left the safety of the oil house and went to his aid but was herself swept away. Keeper Small awoke some time later lying on the wreckage of the boathouse, but his heroic wife succumbed to her injuries.

Bird Island Lighthouse was built in 1818 near the entrance to Sippican Harbor. In 1842, Keeper John Clark noted that the dwelling was "tolerable comfortable" and that there was a well but no water. Thus he was forced to travel daily to the mainland for his needs. In the 1880s as the harbor in Marion was bustling with commerce, the light gained in importance until the early 1900s when it was discontinued. (D.C. Keyes view, author's collection.)

This third lighthouse at Cuttyhunk was constructed in the 1890s to replace the aging wooden 1860s light and included a round, wooden tower connected to a six-room keeper's house. Although Cuttyhunk is relatively small, it lies in the well-traveled passage between Buzzards Bay and Vineyard Sound and thus required a reliable light of the fifth order. In 1602 when Gosnold landed from the bark *Concord*, Cuttyhunk became the site of the first English colonization.

120

Cleveland Ledge Lighthouse guards the southern approach to the Cape Cod Canal. The light was built on a concrete caisson and towed to the site in 1940. In 1944 the Coast Guard keepers on Cleveland Ledge would be severely tested as a dangerous hurricane swept north. As waves came crashing in, skylights and windows broke, and the water began to rise. However, the Coast Guardsmen persevered, and the light was never extinguished. (Official Coast Guard photo, author's collection.)

Cuttyhunk Island is one of the Elizabeth chain of islands stretching southwest from Falmouth. The unusual 1889 Life-Saving/Coast Guard Station here was designed by Albert Bibb and was a one-of-a-kind shingle style. The octagonal watch tower and arched boat room doors combine to give the appearance of a cottage, and a most attractive one at that. Shown here in the 1920s, the station stood near the east end of the island and saw numerous wrecks.

On August 27, 1924, while beating northward ahead of a gale, the bark *Wanderer* grounded on the rocks off Cuttyhunk Island. Fortunately, no lives were lost, but shipping and the towns along the coast were hard hit, and a number of losses were suffered. In time, such sailing vessels would become a memory of the past as steam and diesel power would take over.

Coast Guardsmen in the 1930s use a caterpillar tractor to tow the surfboat back to the boatroom following a drill. In the early years, life-savers were fortunate when they were able to keep or borrow draft animals to aid them in pulling their apparatus through the soft sand. In some areas mules were used, but on Cape Cod horses were preferred. In later years tractors, and after WW II, Jeeps were used for this task.

At the turn of the 20th century, the Second Lighthouse District had four lighthouse tenders in service, the *Verbina*, *Mayflower*, *Azalea*, and the *Myrtle*. A typical tender of this era was a steel screw steamer, coal burning side wheeled with a walking beam engine. Tenders were used to deliver fuel and supplies to lighthouses and light vessels within the district and to repair buoys and navigational aids. As an example, in 1891 the *Azalea* was employed 265 days and repaired or painted 110 buoys, delivered 631 tons of coal, 194 loads of rations and supplies, and steamed 10,415 miles. Another duty of the tender was to transport the district lighthouse inspector to each station for his periodic inspection. When the inspector was aboard, the tender would fly the inspector's white triangular pennant which would alert the keeper that the inspector was on board. Keepers and families would always watch for this pennant, for it meant that all must be in order and polished to perfection. Shown is an unidentified tender, possibly the *Verbina*, at the Light-House Depot in New Bedford *c*. 1880s. (R.R. Topham photograph, author's collection.)

Ned Point Light in Mattapoisett was erected in 1837 and rebuilt again in 1888. Edward Rowe Snow wrote in his book *Famous New England Lighthouses* that during a period of government economy, the light was listed in the local newspaper to the "lowest" bidder, a mistake they quickly remedied when 1¢ was bid. The dwelling was floated by barge to Wings Neck, where it became the assistant keeper's home. (H.S. Hutchinson view, author's collection.)

Clark's Point or Butler's Flats Light was located on Clark's Neck in 1804 at the request of the New Bedford captains. As the area became more active, Congress approved a beacon on Butler's Flats and the Clark's Point Light was extinguished. Three successive generations of the locally known Baker family served as keepers of these lights from 1872 until the 1940s, which was quite an accomplishment.

Here the Vineyard Sound Light Vessel No. 73 and Hen and Chickens Shoals No. 49 sit lined up at Homer's Wharf at the Light-House Depot in New Bedford in November of 1932. The vessel tied up beyond may be a Light-House Service tender, as the New Bedford Depot serviced the lighthouses and buoys throughout the area. (Photo by James E. Reynolds, author's collection.)

1523   Dumpling Light at Entrance to Buzzards Bay, New Bedford, Mass.

In February 1905 the Nantucket Light Vessel was steaming back to her station after laying over in New Bedford for repairs, when off Mishawm Point, the ice became so thick that she was forced to drop anchor. As the ice increased, she began to be dragged and stranded near the Dumpling Rock Light. It required two tugs, the tender *Azalea*, and the U.S. Gunboat *Hist* to drag her off the sand. (H.S. Hutchinson view, author's collection.)

By about 1910 the Life-Saving Service began converting from pulling (oar) boats to the new motorized lifeboats. Though engines were still in their early stages of development they afforded the life-savers the ability to extend their range and to be less exhausted upon arrival. Thus they would be better able to perform their rescue duties. Shown is a Coast Guard boat about 1935, probably a 34-foot motorized lifeboat.

Among the drills that Life-Saving Service personnel were required to perform was the surfboat capsize drill. The ability to right a surfboat overturned by the sea was most important to the life-saver's survival as evidenced by the disaster off Monomoy in 1902, and crews became adept at this procedure. Shanks and York, in their book *The U.S. Life-Saving Service*, note that the service record was just 13 seconds to right an overturned boat.

126

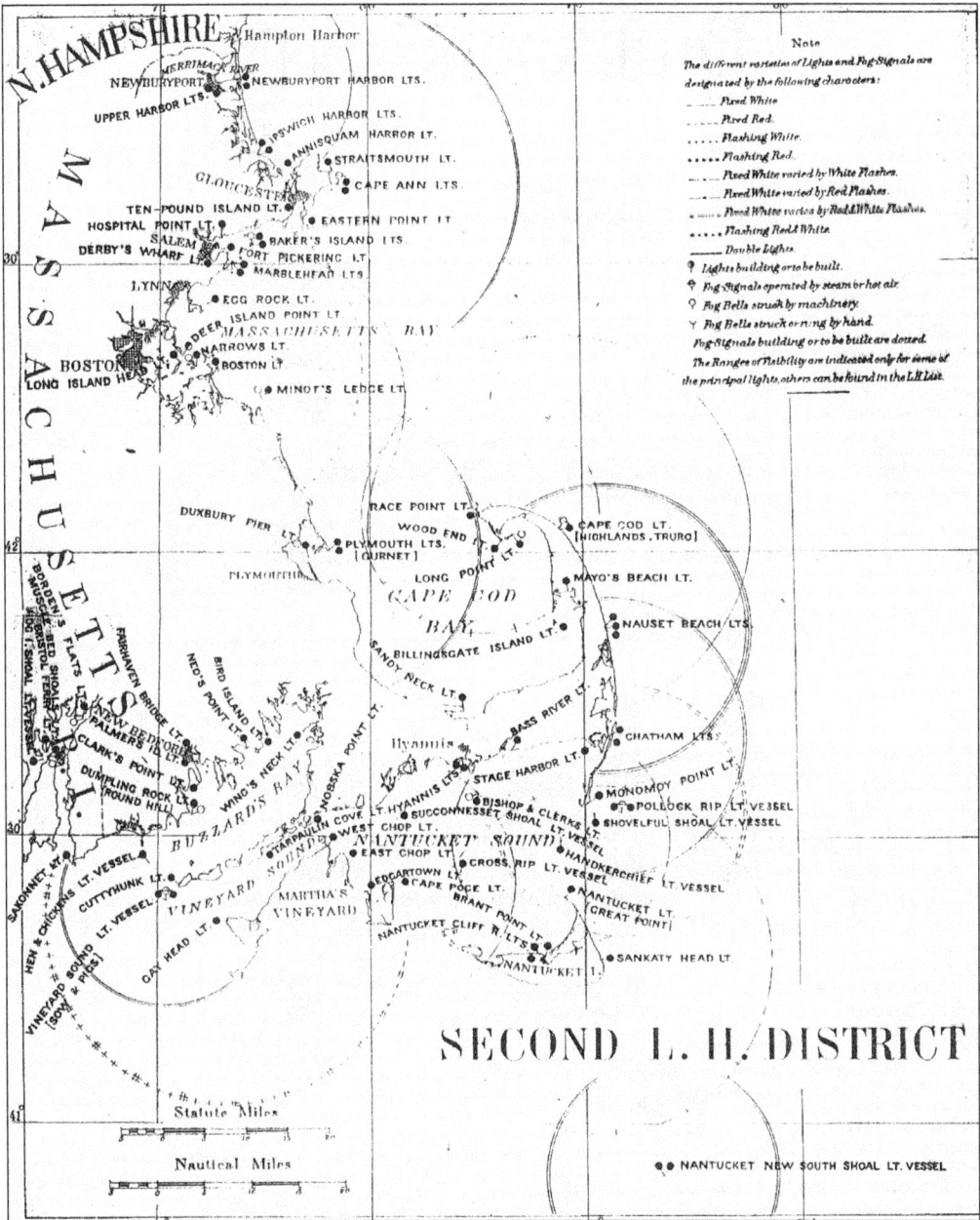

(From Annual Report of the Light-House Board, 1888.)

BIBLIOGRAPHY

Information from the following sources have been used in researching this volume:

Carmen, Ruth. *Storm Child*. New York: John C. Yorston Publishing Co., 1937.

Clark, Admont G. *Lighthouses of Cape Cod—Martha's Vineyard—Nantucket*. East Orleans: Parnassus Imprints, 1992.

Dalton, J.W. *The Life Savers of Cape Cod*. Boston: The Barta Press, 1902.

Holland, Francis Ross, Jr., *America's Lighthouses—Their Illustrated History Since 1716*. Brattleboro: The Stephen Greene Press, 1972.

Howe, Mark Anthony DeWolfe. *The Humane Society of the Commonwealth of Massachusetts*. Boston: Massachusetts Humane Society, 1918.

Kimball, Sumner I., *Joshua James*. Boston: American Unitarian Association, 1909.

_____, *Report of the General Superintendent of the Life-Saving Service Relative to the Claims of W. A. Newell as the Originator of the System of the Life-Saving Service of the United States*. Washington: Senate Document No. 270, May 18, 1898.

Lombard, Asa Cobb Paine, Jr. *East of Cape Cod*. New Bedford: Reynolds DeWitt, 1976.

na. *Destruction of Minot's Ledge Lighthouse*. Gleason's Pictorial Drawing Room Companion. May 10, 1851.

na. *The Life-Saving Service*. Harper's Weekly. March 27, 1886.

na. *The United States Life Saving Service*. Scientific American Supplement. February 21, 1891.

na. *The Building and the Exhibit of the United States Life-Saving Service*. Historical Register of the Centennial Exposition. Pary VII., 1876.

O'Connor, William D. *Heroes of the Storm*. Boston: Houghton, Mifflin and Company, 1904.

Quinn, William P. *Shipwrecks Around Cape Cod*. Orleans: Lower Cape Publishing, 1973.

Robinson, J.H. *106 Views of Nantucket*. Nantucket Island: J.H. Robinson, 1911.

Shanks, Ralph and Wick York. *The U.S. Life-Saving Service*. Petaluma: Costano Books, 1996.

Snow, Edward Rowe. *The Islands of Boston Harbor*. Andover: The Andover Press, July 1936.

_____, *Famous New England Lighthouses*. Boston: The Yankee Publishing Co., October 1945.

Stackpole, Edouard A. *Life Saving Nantucket*. Nantucket Island: Stern Majestic, 1972.

Thompson, Frederic L. *The Lightships of Cape Cod*. Northborough: Kenrick A. Claflin & Son, 1996.

Thoreau, Henry David. *Cape Cod*. Boston: Houghton Mifflin Co., 1893.

U.S. Coast Guard. *Annual Reports*. Washington: G.P.O., 1914–1926.

U.S. Life-Saving Service. *Annual Reports*. Washington: G.P.O., 1876–1914.

_____, *Mortar and Beach-Apparatus Drill*. Washington: G.P.O., 1880.

_____, *Regulations for the Government of the Life-Saving Service of the United States*. Washington: G.P.O., 1899.

U.S. Light-House Establishment [Service]. *Annual Reports*. Washington: G.P.O., 1846–1938.

Willoughby, Malcom F. *Lighthouses of New England*. Boston: T.O. Metcalf Company, 1929.

Wood, Vincent L. *Plum Island Recollections*. Newbury: Newburyport Press, 1995.

For additional reading, the above original vintage titles and many others are available from Kenrick A. Claflin & Son Nautical Antiques, 1227 Pleasant Street, Worcester, MA 01602.

For still additional information about our lighthouses and life-saving and Coast Guard stations, please contact the following organizations:

United States Life-Saving Service Heritage Association, P.O. Box 75, Caledonia, MI 49316-0075

United States Lighthouse Society, 244 Kearny Street, San Francisco, CA 94108

The New England Lighthouse Foundation, P.O. Box 1690, Wells, ME 04090

www.ingramcontent.com/pod-product-compliance
Lightning Source LLC
Chambersburg PA
CBHW080900100426
42812CB00007B/2101